Endorsements

William Coker, who has served churches in four states with the support of his wife, Ann, has produced a lucid account of the gospel he has proclaimed, as reflected in the sermons preached while pastor of the World Gospel Church in Terre Haute, Indiana. Based on the keynote text of I Corinthians 1:18f, "the preaching of the cross is to those who perish foolishness, but to those who are being saved it is the power of God," he has developed a deep focus on a church built on the power of the cross that embraces a community where that faith is breaking down walls to reach the lost for Christ.

The core of this message shows how the church is called to reflect the redeemed God/human relationship, transformed once and for all by Christ's work on Calvary that brought victory in our human struggle with sin and condemnation. For Coker, the preaching for apostolic revival becomes the key to unlock the magnitude of that redemptive life for the people of God.

This reviewer also found insight when reading this message from an inverted perspective: rather than beginning with the church and its message, we could envision beginning with God and his love for a lost humanity. The church then becomes the center for that life changing meeting of God with His people who need Him. This points to the vital relationship that exists between a person's will and the love of God. Since our Lord created us as children with free will to accept or reject Him as our heavenly Father, the critical question in the mission of the church becomes: Will people will to receive and live through the wondrous gospel Christ our Head offers us? If He had created us without volition, there would have been no capacity for sin but also no liberty to worship and love Him and one another. What a risk God took out of love for us, to create us in His own image, to become a people who could turn from ignoring Him under Satan's temptation, to serving Him out of allowing ourselves to enter into His blessed fellowship (the church). Either way we look at it, the church is where we become members of His body, so as a person each of us may become part of the redeemed community, the church, whose common worship of our Lord strengthens each of our personal lives in living out His life in us, for the life of the world.

Bill Coker's faithful preaching and modeling of this message for his people is beautifully set forth in this volume, edited in his honor by his helpmate, Ann. To God be the glory, and may many turn to Him through this testimony of how the church can be the church, after all.

Dr. William Coker has been one of the most influential Bible teachers in my life. I have listened to many sermons, retreat talks on grace, and biblical study in small groups. This new book of his is truly deep and impactful. I suggest that you take your time and read with intention. It is packed with living truth. The chapter on prayer spoke to my heart. How the local church pales in comparison to the fervor of the early church when it comes to prayer. I loved the line that said that the disciples had confidence in prayer because they had confidence in the One to whom they were praying.

Do we today have such complete confidence in our Heavenly Father or do we try to tell Him how things should be? Our western individualism has caused us to act like we can live life without His divine guidance. No wonder our country is in the state it is today! Dr. Coker's book, *Let the Church Be the Church* is an amazing book to inspire us all to be stronger Christians as we deepen our relationship with our Father. It is a must read!

From stories of David as a young boy, to the shepherds who came to see the baby Jesus, to our Lord's analogy of Himself as the good shepherd, we learn that God is in the business of herding sheep. In his book, *Let the Church be the Church: Participate in God's Miracle,* Dr. William Coker describes the miracle of how God has shepherded His church to proclaim the gospel to the nations for nearly 2000 years.

Dr. Coker issues a clarion call for the church to reclaim its God-ordained mission. He begins by identifying the problem of our times, stating: "I'm frustrated, not because a sinful world is out there, but because a weak church is not responding to the challenge of our age."

The heart of the book lays out the Three Ps: that Christians, acting in concert with the Body of Christ, be a Praying church, a Pentecostal church, and a Proclaiming church. Eschewing flashy marketing schemes and concert-like worship services, Coker calls on us to be the hands and feet of Christ, reaching out in love to a fallen world. That's the blueprint he lays out to *Let the Church be the Church.* If you are looking for wisdom to cause you to contemplate the role God wants you to play in the miracle of His church, this book is for you!

—David L. Lantz, Author of *Think Like Jesus, Lead Like Moses: Leadership Lessons from the Wilderness Crucible*, Indianapolis, Indiana

It was in 1979, over 40 years ago, when I was a student at Asbury Theological Seminary that I first met Bill and Ann Coker. Dr. Coker was then the Dean of Asbury College and Ann was on the editorial team at *Good News Magazine* where my wife, Cynthia, also worked. Fast forward 14 years later, having been newly appointed to pastor a church in Terre Haute, Indiana, Cynthia and I were happy to learn that Bill and Ann were also in Terre Haute, pastoring a healthy, mission-minded, evangelical church. Bill has used his life and voice to help strengthen and encourage those whom he has served. I can testify that he lived what he preached.

In this book, he discusses not only the needs of today's church, but gives helpful examples as to how to keep the church focused on Jesus and the Word of God. This book is a helpful and refreshing compass that can be used to help guide any church leader through these stormy times. Throughout the book, one truth comes through: when we major on the things we share in common, and thus minimize our differences, churches are more united and the world looks on with greater admiration. In each chapter, Bill Coker guides the reader with positional steps to *Let the Church Be the Church.*

—**Aaron Wheaton, retired UM Pastor and**
  Musician, Terre Haute, Indiana

Dr. Coker answers King David's question. (See Psalm 11:3.) When the foundations are being destroyed, only the righteous can *do* something about it. That's why I count it a profound privilege, and even an imperative, to recommend his important book. William Coker's messages are born of a pastor's compassionate heart, a theologian's keen eye, and a culture influencer's relevance to today's issues. Reading his powerful sermons has caused me to reevaluate my own priorities and methodologies as a Christian leader. I think Dr. Coker's messages will change your life, as well as those you touch. Read it, wrestle afresh with its transforming truths, and then buy it as a gift for your family, friends, and especially your pastor.

Only when we return to foundational biblical principles, so wonderfully laid out by Dr. William Coker, can we ever restore the foundations of our families, churches, and communities.

—Dr. Robert Petterson, Founder and President, Legacy Imperative, Inc., Naples, Florida (from Foreword)

The Church is Christianity's greatest miracle... and Christianity's greatest challenge. In this insightful book with wisdom gleaned from decades of studying, teaching, preparing and delivering sermons, and being a pastor, Bill Coker dives into the calling of the Church to connect Christ to a practical, living faith for believers.

The church is where we learn about God. The church is where we experience His unconditional love through the life, death, and resurrection of His Son, Jesus Christ. The church is where we learn how the Holy Spirit of God leads us. And the church invites all to come and experience the difference being a disciple of Jesus Christ makes in a person's life.

That is the church at its best, fulfilling the mission it was designed for when the apostles were chosen, and disciples came on board over 2000 years ago. Unfortunately, as Bill points out, the church doesn't always live up to its calling. Why? Because the church is comprised of imperfect human beings who are called to do God's perfect will. And at times the church gets it wrong, because our imperfections become manifest.

People are seeking to find a purpose to life. The secular world steps in with its siren calls of self-fulfillment, pleasures, power, and wealth, yet disappoints time and again. Into this breach, Bill contends, should step the church, because providing meaning for life is its divine calling.

The conundrum we face is how to make that happen when so many over the centuries have been hurt or misled by the church. We can all list the ways: judging outsiders and insiders, beating people legalistically over the head with the Bible, accumulating wealth, church leaders becoming intoxicated with their own power, even taking advantage of those who trusted them. The sad results are that hurting people still are hurting, with an emptiness that never goes away.

However, despair not, for there is hope for the church. The journey to allow the church to be the church is not shrouded in mystery. Bill shows us step-by-practical step how the church can be restored to the redemptive purpose to which Christ called it. First, acknowledge that Jesus Christ is Lord and Head of the Church. Jesus leads us by His Holy Spirit to be unified in Him. And we accept that unity does not mean unanimity. We have differences among us and always will, but we can all be tethered to Christ as the center of the Church. We must pray and seek God's will, measuring our decisions, teachings, ministry, and lives against the divine guidance of the Holy Spirit. We must worship God regularly, both individually and corporately, glorifying Christ in our thoughts, words, and deeds. And we must proclaim the saving grace of our Lord Jesus Christ.

Will it be easy to let the Church be the Church? No, but Bill points out that being church members is a team sport that we all participate in. And if we do, the church will once again blossom as it fulfills its divine potential, comforting the hurting, healing the wounded, encouraging the discouraged, embracing the sanctity of human life, and most of all, offering saving grace to all as we make disciples in all nations.

—Bart Colwell, United Methodist Pastor and Bank President and CEO

Let the Church Be the Church opened my mind to the idea of the Church as one of God's greatest miracle. It's confounding to imagine the Creator of the universe turning over His mission to His children. Here are two samples to entice you to read the book.

"In my floor plan for a church, there are no walls. We need a church where anybody and everybody can feel welcome to come in."

"Prayer: Our Father, we pray that You would stir our hearts to want to build Your kind of a church—the kind in which people can come with all our differences, with all our similarities, with all our likes and dislikes, and with all our preferences and ambitions. For we find at the foot of the cross of Christ only one cause transcending all else—the great love of God shed abroad in our hearts through the Holy Spirit. Through Christ our Lord we ask. Amen."

—John Matthew Walker, Physician and Author, Indianapolis, Indiana

Let the CHURCH Be the CHURCH

Participate in God's Miracle

Rev. William B. Coker, PhD

with Ann L. Coker, editor

Foreword by Dr. Robert Petterson

EABooks Publishing
Your Partner In Publishing

Cover design and chapter format by Robin Black
Author photos used with permission by Scott Kokoska
Cover art by iStockphoto/DigitalStorm

EABooks Publishing
www.eabookspublishing.com

Let the Church Be the Church
by Rev. William B. Coker, PhD
with Ann L. Coker, editor

ISBN: 978-1-955309-88-2

To
congregations
in Mississippi,
Kentucky,
Indiana,
and other churches
where God's ministry
has taken us

Table of Contents

Foreword

by Dr. Robert Petterson,
founder and CEO of Legacy Imperative

Tsunamis of change are crashing in upon us, smashing foundational truths, values, and institutions to smithereens. Views and behaviors considered abnormal five to ten years ago are the new normal today. Most distressingly, we are rapidly losing the next generations to the Faith that sustained and nurtured those who came before us.

The dizzying changes in our digital age begs a question asked by King David three thousand years ago: "When the foundations are being destroyed, what can the righteous do?" (Psalm 11:3). The easy answer is to point our fingers at cultural forces and influencers attacking and dismantling those things Christians hold dear, or to become warriors in the culture battles that rip our families, churches, and world apart.

I believe Dr. William Coker has better answers grounded in the unshakable truths of Scripture, and yet more relevant than tomorrow's headlines. Solutions to shoring up the foundations won't be found in the White House, courthouse, schoolhouse, movie house, statehouse, or houses of Congress. They are found in the church house, your house, and my house. Dr. Coker comes right to the point in the title of his book: *Let the Church Be the Church*.

If the light goes out in the churches, or those who belong to them, the darkness in our world will become that of outer hell. In his much-needed book, Dr Coker gets us back to basics that have long been forgotten in the churches' mad rush to fill pews and coffers by appealing to the spirit of our postmodern culture. He cuts to the chase by taking us back to the New Testament Church that transformed the pagan Greco-Roman world. The author shows us how it can happen yet again, if we return to the basics he shares from the Scriptures.

Dr. Coker answers King David's question. When the foundations are being destroyed, only the righteous can *do* something about it. That's why I count it a profound privilege, and even an imperative, to recommend his important book. William Coker's messages are born of a pastor's compassionate heart, a theologian's keen eye, and a culture influencer's relevance to today's issues. Reading his powerful sermons has caused me to reevaluate my own priorities and methodologies as a Christian leader. I think Dr. Coker's messages will change your life, as well as those you touch. Read it, wrestle afresh with its transforming truths, and then buy it as a gift for your family, friends, and especially your pastor.

Only when we return to foundational biblical principles, so wonderfully laid out by Dr. William Coker, can we ever restore the foundations of our families, churches, and communities.

Introduction

by Ann L. Coker

What is central in our lives? Some thing or some one? Christ is central to our faith, and the church is (or should be) the place where we connect Christ with a living faith. That's because the Church universal is the living embodiment of Christ in the world.

How does the church fit into our focus, into the priorities of our lifestyles? If Christ is the central focus of our lives, it is predominately in the church where we learn about the centrality of Christ, as we see from the apostle Paul's letters that addressed the church in Corinth.

In this collection of Bill's messages on the church, my husband/pastor emphasizes the issue of Christ being the central focus of our faith, and the church being the foundational means of learning about Christ and faith.

Several times you will read that Bill firmly believes the Church is the greatest miracle throughout history. The virgin birth and the resurrection, while both miracles, would be an easy accomplishment for our sovereign Creator God. But the Church is also a miracle, because it involves people and has remarkably lasted for over 2000 years. While the church has undergone persecution in every century and continues today, it has survived and even flourished.

A word about these messages formatted into book chapters. This is a collection, not a series. They are gleaned over several years, and while most are from sermons presented at World Gospel Church in Terre Haute, Indiana, Bill also preached some during special meetings at other churches. The order does not follow any chronological order. Their arrangement suits the content, including two divided into sections. Each builds upon the previous message and concludes with one in which Bill builds a church without walls.

Our prayer is that you will come away with a greater appreciation for the Church universal and participate in the miracle of your own local church.

CHAPTER ONE

The Central Focus of the Church

1 Corinthians 1:18–31

"The cross is the symbol of Christianity, and the cross speaks of death and separation, never of compromise. . . . The cross is the essence of all that is extreme and final. The message of Christ is a call across a gulf from death to life, from sin to righteousness, and from Satan to God" (A. W. Tozer, *The Set of the Sail*).[1]

I invite your attention to Paul's first letter to the Corinthians, chapter one, beginning with verse eighteen, closing with verse thirty-one.

For the message of the cross is foolishness to those who are perishing, but to us who are being saved it is the power of God. For it is written: "I will destroy the wisdom of the wise; the intelligence of the intelligent I will frustrate." Where is the wise person? Where is the teacher of the law? Where is the philosopher of this age? Has not God made foolish the wisdom of the world? For since in the wisdom of God the world through its wisdom did not know him, God was pleased through the foolishness of what was preached to save those who believe. Jews demand signs and Greeks look for wisdom, but we preach Christ crucified: a stumbling block to Jews and foolishness to Gentiles, but to those whom God has called, both Jews and Greeks, Christ the power of God and the wisdom of God. For the foolishness of God is wiser than human wisdom, and the weakness of God is stronger than human strength. Brothers and sisters, think of what you were when you were called. Not many of you were wise by human standards; not many were influential; not many were of noble birth. But God chose the foolish things of the world to shame the wise; God chose the weak things of the world to shame the strong. God chose the lowly things of this world and the despised things—and the things that are not—to nullify things that are, so that no one may boast before him. It is because of him that you are in Christ Jesus, who has become for us wisdom from God – that is, our righteousness, holiness and redemption. Therefore, as it is written: "Let the one who boasts boast in the Lord."—1 Corinthians 1:18–31

Suppose the apostle Paul had been asked, "What is central to your life?" Paul would definitely have answered this question with a person: Jesus Christ. In fact, he began his first letter to the Corinthians with an emphasis on Christ being central in the church, before getting to his reasons for writing. You'll notice the early church exhibited a great deal of difficulty, for he wrote of divisions, mentioning the quarreling among them. Before addressing these difficulties, Paul emphasized Christ being central.

Centrality of Christ

Many times in the first chapter Paul made references to our Lord Jesus Christ, God's Son. Before Paul ever addressed the issues that divided people, he emphasized that which united them or ought to unite them in Christian faith. That one criteria was the centrality of Jesus.

In his book, *Sources of the Self*, Charles Taylor[2] made an interesting statement. I'm putting what he said into a Christian context. These are not his words, but my extrapolation: We are defined by our commitment and identification with God's Son, our Lord Jesus Christ. This frames what we determine is good or valuable, or what we ought not to do or to oppose. Taylor didn't refer to Christ or any religious connection; he wrote about the sources of the self. His point was this: If you ask the question, "Who am I?" the answer is what we are committed to and with

what we identify ourselves. This theory is basic to
how we make decisions in our lives; and those decisions are dictated by the convictions we have or the
identifications we assume.

According to Taylor, if I'm to know who I am,
then I have to know what my commitments are and
how I identify myself. That's true in a secular sense,
but it's also true in a religious sense. As Christians
that's certainly true, for it's what Paul wanted the
Corinthians to understand. If we're going to identify
who we are, ultimately we come back to our center,
the focal point in Jesus Christ. It was true in Paul's
day, and it's still true today. As Christians we cannot
focus on denominations; we cannot focus on varying
doctrinal distinctives. Our commitment is to Christ
and our identification is with Christ.

Paul was saying: "Now you folks are quarreling
about whether you're going to follow this pastor or
another pastor." In his words, "One of you says,—
I follow Paul'; another, 'I follow Apollos'; another.
'I follow Cephas'; still another, 'I follow Christ'"
(1 Corinthians 1:12). Christ is not divided. The center for our faith is singular, and our relationships
hinge on one another. In this same passage, Paul
talked about God bringing us into the fellowship of
His Son (v. 9).

It's the word "fellowship" I want to take out of
the text for you, because the Greek word, *koinonia*,

comes from a word meaning "common." The New Testament was written in *Koine* Greek, which was business Greek, the common Greek of the streets. *Koinonia* is a business term, and it means individuals have a relationship with one another because they share in common the same goal. In business we would say partners have a relationship with one another because they are bonded to the same business. They are partners; that's what *koinonia* is. When God brings us into fellowship with His Son, the unity that binds us together is not in similarities we may share, but in the centrality of Jesus himself.

The quarrels the Corinth church members had were not only unnecessary, they were wrong. If you're followers of Apollos, or Cephas, or Paul . . . "Hey wait a minute," Paul emphasized, "Was I crucified for you? Were you baptized in my name? I'm thankful I baptized only a few of you, and I don't want you to think for a moment you were baptized in my name." It all comes back to the central focus: Christ alone.

Focus on the Cross

As we continue to read chapter one of First Corinthians, the centrality of Christ begins to focus on the cross of Christ. When I began my ministry I had no background in theological studies, so I began to read from a number of different authors. One author, A.B. Simpson,[3] asked why the cross is the center of the Christian faith rather than baptism. He answered his own question. Baptism, after all, does represent the resurrection and it's the emphasis in Christian faith, for we are resurrected together with Christ. He wasn't saying that's how it ought to be, but if you think about it logically, maybe that's the better symbol. However, the symbol of the church as we recognize and see it in church after church is not baptism but the cross.

I hear Paul saying: "God did not send me forth to baptize people, but to preach the cross of Christ." Paul preferred not to preach with words of eloquent wisdom, less the cross of Christ be nullified, made null and void, lose out and come across as nothing. Paul looked at the centrality of Christ and saw beyond to the cross that made a difference in people's lives. As we read the New Testament, we cannot escape the significance of the cross. If we focus on the centrality of Jesus, what we discover is the cross of Christ right at the center of the gospel that's preached in His name.

Think with me about the cross of Christ. Churches have crosses on the walls of their buildings or on steeples. We see them frequently, but I wonder how often we stop and ponder why they're displayed and nicely lighted, so we're attracted to them. What's the point? Why on the steeples? What is a cross trying to emphasize? What is the significance Paul and other New Testament writers saw? And why did the cross become the focal point of Jesus' ministry? Was not His resurrection important? Obviously. Certainly. He was declared to be the Son of God with power by the resurrection of the dead. I'm not down playing anything.

Sign of the Cross

When we look at the gospel of Christ, the cross immediately jumps out, and that's what Paul saw. Now what's the truth here? When you look at the cross, you see it's the sign of our redemption. But before we go any further, it is also the sign of our sinfulness. We are sinners.

Evelyn Underhill wrote the best book on worship I've ever read, simply titled *Worship*.[4] She wrote about the crucifix in Catholic and Orthodox traditions. I'd never thought about that; I grew up in a Methodist church and our crosses were not crucifixes, they are crosses. Underhill stated how the crucifix is essential to understanding the significance of the cross of Christ. Her words so impressed me that I went out and bought a crucifix. I hung it on the wall of my study at home.

When my older brother visited me, he looked at that crucifix on the wall and asked, "Why have you got that up there? That's Catholic."

I said, "I have it there because it reminds me of my own sinfulness. It isn't Catholic; it's Christian."

When we look at the cross, the first thought that ought to occur to all of us is why the cross is central. It's not because of what Christ did in and of itself. It's *why* He died, and the reason is to be found in the fact that we're sinners. We're lost and undone.

We have only to look at the news briefly until we see our sinfulness, and not only in wars across Afghanistan, Iraq, or Lebanon. One day I read in the newspaper about the fifteenth murder in Indianapolis, Indiana, in a matter of a week or more. It's startling. It's everywhere: man's inhumanity to man. We're self-centered, self-focused, grasping for self; what I want cancels out everything else. But when you stand at the cross and look at it, the first word from the cross is our sinfulness. The reason we need the cross is because we're sinners.

I listened to an interview with Henry Blackaby[5] as he talked about revival in the church. He said the problem with us in the church is we pray for those sinners outside the church who need to repent and come to God. We think about how the world could change if sinners would get converted. Blackaby said the problem is we don't begin at the right place. We ought to begin with ourselves. There's enough sin to be repented of—represented in church services on Sunday mornings—so that a revival could begin right now, here in church. You have to ask the question, "Will it begin any other place?"

I've read about revivals through the history of the church. I've noticed they didn't happen because a group of sinners got together and said, "Hey, why don't we have revival?" Revival starts in the church and exactly how Blackaby described it. We see our sin, we understand our need for forgiveness, and when that is taken care of, then the grace of God, the power of God, works within the people of God to the point where we impact the world.

Now let me ask a question, and it's not to put any of us down. I'm including myself. If we look at the church at large, what would happen in our towns if two hundred churches this day had people gather together and bow down on our faces? We would remember our spiritual lack and admit our faults that keep us from being what God has intended for us.

If we could resolve those barriers, the church would be stronger and purer. Then the Spirit of God would move in such power the world would be changed. I believe this change could happen in your church and my church. To go further, if it began with you and me, then the power of God would move in the people of God to impact a nation. I know it to be true, because it's happened numerous times in the past.

God's Love Behind the Cross

We look at the cross and say, "What's the significance of the cross that it should be at the center of the gospel of Christ?" It's because He came, because we're sinners, and we need to repent and come back to God. But it doesn't only emphasize our sinfulness; it also declares the magnificent love of God for each one of us. Why do I have a crucifix on my wall? Because I'm reminded Christ died for my sins, but also in His death I find that "God so loved the world that he gave his one and only Son, that whoever believes in him shall not perish but have eternal life" (John 3:16). Christ's death on the cross not only expressed the fact that I'm a sinner who needs to be saved; it also tells me God loves and desired me. I belong to Him and with His people.

Paul wrote to a church divided on many different issues; and he simply said, "Let's begin with Jesus. Let's put our central focus upon Christ; and as we look to Him, what we're going to see here in the cross of Christ is the secret for what will transform the church and make it a genuine fellowship of believers." This emphasis underscores our need for repentance, but it also underscores our need to accept the love God offers us. The cross says, "God loves you"; but it also asks, "What is your response?"

Good News of the Cross

When Paul talked about the work of the cross, he recognized that many people reject it. He wrote: "The message of the cross is foolishness to those who are perishing, but to us who are being saved it is the power of God" (1 Corinthians 1:18). Yes, some people look and say, "This is nonsense." I don't know what Paul faced in his day, but maybe he dealt with people who thought the greatest enemy we face as human beings is death.

Later in that same letter to the church in Corinth (chapter 15), Paul wrote about death being the great enemy that needs to be defeated, but here he's preaching a Christ who died. If the greatest enemy we face in life is death, how can the fact that a man died be good news for us? This dichotomy underscores what we all experience. We've buried too many of our loved ones, friends, and neighbors to think that a man dying could be good news. People looked the cross and said, "This is foolishness. How could this possibly be good?"

Jews Want Signs

Paul became more particular. He talked about the Jews. For them the cross was a stumbling block. They were not looking for a Messiah who would die on a cross. They wanted a Messiah who would establish the nation of Israel, a Messiah who would restore the kingdom they once knew under David, a Messiah who would triumph on a throne. They listened to Paul and his message of Christ, and they called it "a stumbling block" (1:23). The Greek word here is *scandalous*. It's as if Paul said: "This is a scandal. This we cannot accept. There's no way we see this as God's answer for us."

Paul said the Jews looked for signs. It's as if God came to Abraham and said, "Look, Abraham, I want to make a covenant with you. I'm going to give to your seed all of the land you see before you. This is to be your nation; I give it to you." Abraham listened to the covenant God was making with him and asked: "How can I know I will possess it? Give me a sign. Show me proof so I will know this covenant is valid, that it's true." (See Genesis 15.)

Later when Jesus came, the Jews said to Jesus: "You claim to be the Messiah. What sign will you show us?" (See Matthew 12:38; 16:1.) He had been doing all kinds of signs, but what were they looking for? They wanted *their* sign. Do this, and they would know He was the Messiah. Anyone ever pray that way? "Oh God, if you do this I'll know You're real." Some of us are still waiting for Him to do something special and we'll know He cares. To the Jewish people we could say, "Wait a minute; you have missed the whole point." There's something deeper, more than showing us a sign.

Years ago a great evangelistic movement developed in America called Power Evangelism.[6] Because it was built on our need for a powerful movement of God to be evidenced in signs and wonders, I thought it was a miscue. Are signs and wonders the proof we need of our belief in God? Do miracles prove God? Then I found myself thinking: *What if a person born blind came to the altar? We could lay hands on that person and immediately see healing. Then we'd have a great revival.* About a minute later, when I screwed my head back on, I thought, *That's nonsense.*

The problem was not that Jesus had not done signs; the Jews wanted a different sign. "Give us another sign." For us today, God has answered prayers on numerous occasions, yet we find ourselves saying: "God give me another sign and I'll know." Faith is created by trusting God, not by any sign He does.

I'll give you a crude example, but since it's up-to-date I'm using it. One problem we have now is sexual activity among teens. I read where one person said, "Young lady, if your boyfriend says to you, prove that you love me, it's time to get out of the car and walk home." You could turn it around and say, "Prove you love me by not asking for sex." How do you prove your love for someone? How do I prove to my wife that I love her? What does she have to do to prove she loves me? Instead, isn't our love built on the covenant we made to each other?

Paul believed preaching the cross holds the power of God. Isn't it true when we turn to the cross, we don't find good advice? The cross is transforming power in your life and in mine. When we come to God, isn't our hope born in faith and sustained by practicing our faith? If you're waiting for God to give you a sign, He's waiting for you to trust Him. We have a rational conviction that God is. He made us, and He has reached out to us in love demonstrated by Christ's life, death, and resurrection.

Greeks Seek Wisdom

"Jews demand signs and Greeks look for wisdom" (1 Corinthians 1:22). Every Greek in Paul's day knew the names of Socrates, Aristotle, Plato, and Epicurus. These were the well-known philosophers. They were the big guns who came up with philosophical theories about life. In Paul's day, we're told in Acts 17:19–21, people gathered on the Areopagus to discuss the latest theory. Tickle our ears with the newest philosophy. The major topic was the philosophy of Stoicism, which touted the greatest of all goods was virtue—to help individuals hone their virtues of character. And it was more important than our passions, for reason governs a total disinterest in anything external. The Epicureans disagreed and presented happiness as the greatest good, and they were not talking about a good time. They desired peace of mind and satisfaction with life. And incidentally, they didn't believe in God.

Then came Paul who proclaimed Jesus who died on a cross; and this crucified man is the Savior, Redeemer of the world. They laughed at Paul on Mars Hill. They rejected his message and said, "No, that's folly. We want wisdom, like Plato or Aristotle." Paul said God cannot be found by man's wisdom. God in His wisdom disclosed Himself in a way that's beyond your wisdom and mine.

Refocusing on the Cross

We look back and think, *That was then, but let's look at now.* What of our own naturalistic culture where we hear, again and again, there is no God? We think science answers all our questions. But is that true? Diogenes Allen,[7] professor of philosophy at Princeton University, wrote a book titled *Christian Belief in a Postmodern World: The Full Wealth of Conviction.* He wrote about the many questions science cannot answer now or ever. For example, science builds itself on the order of our world, but when you ask, "Why this order and not some other order?" no answers exist. Diogenes Allen came to the conclusion that science has never ruled out the possibility of God.

All of this fluff about evolution (even if it were proven to be true) does not remove the fact there is a God who made it possible. Some people laugh because we talk about miracles, but no scientific reason can disprove a supernatural being who can interject Himself into our world and into our lives. Science has no answer, and good scientists admit this. Others hide behind the so-called science that rules out God's existence. Some say it's folly, but Paul said it is the power of God.

The word of the cross is a self-authenticating word; and if we accept Paul's teaching to the Corinthians, we will agree that the word of the cross is the wisdom of God.

It is the power of God for our inability.

It is the love of God for our sinfulness.

It is the light of God for our darkness.

It is the fullness of God for our emptiness.

No wonder Paul wrote to the Galatians and said, "May I never boast except in the cross of our Lord Jesus Christ" (6:14). Isaac Watts said it thus: "Forbid it, Lord, that I should boast, save in the death of Christ, my God. All the vain things that charm me most, I sacrifice them to His blood."[8]

Paul began a letter to a divided church about the central figure before us: Christ. The central focus we see in Christ is the cross, because it is there He made possible our redemption. Churches in American don't need another new program or another theologian to present various ideas of this, that, or the other. In the lives of us who are Christians, we need to refocus our attention upon Christ and His cross. If we will do that, God will rise up to meet the needs of this age.

Are you frustrated as you read the newspapers or look at the news on TV or the Internet? I'm frustrated, not because a sinful world is out there, but because a weak church is not responding to the challenge of our age. That's you and me. That's your church and my church. Imagine if Paul were writing this letter to us, even though the problems may not be the same. Thinking about what he has said, how do we discover for ourselves that the power of God is in the cross of Christ? He is not nonsense. His message is not folly. Christ has made available the power necessary to bear witness for Him.

I press it closer and more personal. If you've not given your life to Christ, why not? Are you looking for God to do some spectacular miracle?

If Christ on a cross is not enough, nothing else will be enough. Time is precious; and you cannot waste a week of it, a day or moment of it. We all want more time, but all of us have all there is of it. The time for you to decide is now.

Wouldn't it be wonderful if we could begin right now with a sense of the presence of God's outpouring upon our lives? We'd like that. Good. It begins with you. It begins with me. If we want a new life, we certainly do not have to convince God. He gave His Son to die on a cross to give it to us. Consider that for a moment. Think about what Paul wrote—but not about the church, or our community, or the world. What about you and me? Am I where God wants me to be? Are you? Is Henry Blackaby right when he said we need to begin with repentance—in my life, your life—so God can accomplish His purposes?

Prayer: Our heavenly Father, we are grateful beyond words for the sacrifice of Christ on the cross for our sins, for the hope given us through Your Son Jesus, the central focus of new life. You have provided the only way into Your eternal presence through the cross of Christ for our redemption. Forgive us, Lord, through the power of Christ's blood shed for each one of us. We thank You for the confidence which is ours as we accept

Your gift of salvation. We pray for the church at large and for ourselves personally, for we all need Your grace to triumph in faith for daily living. Comfort our hearts and enlarge our faith—until the light of the knowledge of Your glory, which shown in the face of Jesus, shines also in us. We dedicate ourselves to serve You. Hear our prayer, O God, which we offer in the strong name of our Savior, Jesus Christ. Amen.

CHAPTER TWO

Preparing a Church

Luke 24:44–49

"The hard voice of the scribe sounds over evangelicalism, but the Church waits for the tender voice of the saint who has penetrated the veil and has gazed with inward eye upon the wonder that is God" (A.W. Tozer, *The Pursuit of God*).[9]

We focus our thoughts on the last verses of Luke's Gospel, chapter twenty-four, verses forty-four through forty-nine. Luke laid the ground work for what he continued to write in the book of Acts.

He said to them, "This is what I told you while I was still with you: Everything must be fulfilled that is written about me in the Law of Moses, the Prophets and the Psalms." Then he opened their minds so they could understand the Scriptures. He told them, "This is what is written: The Messiah will suffer and rise from the dead on the third day, and repentance for the forgiveness of sins will be preached in his name to all nations, beginning at Jerusalem. You are witnesses of these things. I am going to send you what my Father has promised; but stay in the city until you have been clothed with power from on high."—Luke 24:44–49

One of the greatest miracles in the world is the miracle of the church. I have no difficulty believing a virgin can give birth to a baby, if that is God's will. Resurrections are not difficult for God. He can do those easily. But think of taking people to whom He has given freedom, with the ability to choose to follow or not to follow, and bring them together into one body and make the kind of lasting impression that's taken place for 2000 years. I have to believe this is the greatest miracle in the New Testament, and it continues to be a miracle today.

I don't know how much Jesus sweated over those first disciples; they were not outstanding leaders in the community, only ordinary men. God took simple people, ordinary individuals, and He worked through their lives to touch others and present the message of the gospel. We often observe God taking the ordinary and using it, rather than choosing what we in the world think of as worthy.

Throughout the life of His ministry, Jesus gathered people with whom He shared the gospel. Not only the twelve whom He had chosen to be His apostles, but also other men and women, who from time to time followed and listened as He spoke. In this last chapter of Luke's Gospel, he telescoped forty days into a few verses. It was not something happening one, two, or three times in a solitary evening. It took place over forty days after Jesus' resurrection, as He appeared to the disciples and spent time with them—last minute preparations, if you please. Those men were going to be His witnesses, going out to bring the gospel to the whole world.

When we notice what Luke included, it seems to me, those last words are important. We don't spend our last moments on triviality, so Luke focused on the important, what Jesus wanted to convey, but also what they needed. We have insight into Jesus' last-minute preparations before He handed the ball to the disciples and said: Now run with it. The church was on the verge of being birthed. Jesus must have felt the need to tie together many loose ends, and only 40 days left to make an impression He hoped would guide them for the rest of their lives.

As I reflect on what Jesus said to them, I know how relevant His message is for us today. Out of what Jesus said to His disciples, we can draw many parallels. So we want to think about these final preparations and make the translation into your experience and mine. Jesus made four points as He talked to His disciples.

Laid the Foundation

First, Jesus reviewed the message He had been speaking for three years. We notice Luke recorded twice that in those last days Jesus did something significant. He went back to the Old Testament and laid the foundation for the message to be proclaimed.

Notice when Jesus joined the two men on the road to Emmaus (Luke 24:13–35), they discussed what had happened in Jerusalem. They didn't recognize Him. So they asked (in my words), "Are you a stranger and don't know what happened? Did you not realize what took place in Jerusalem?"

After they finished telling him, Jesus said, "But don't you realize what God has said to us in His word?" He began with the prophets and opened their minds by laying the foundation.

Later with His disciples Jesus said: "Everything must be fulfilled that is written about me in the Law of Moses, the Prophets and the Psalms" (Luke 24:44b).

That's an important phrase, because nowhere else in the New Testament did Jesus join all three Old Testament sections, representing the whole of the Old Testament as the Jewish scholars divided the Scriptures. Jesus grouped the Law of Moses;

the prophecies that began with Samuel through the great prophets and the latter prophets (the minor prophets we call them, though they weren't minor at all); right on into Psalms and the wisdom literature. He said: "Don't you realize these have laid a foundation? What has taken place is foundational to what has been spoken."

Again and again in the writings of the apostles, along with Luke who was not an apostle, they underscored this was to fulfill what had been spoken. In those latter days, Jesus found it imperative for the disciples to go back and understand the foundations had already been laid. God had prepared the nation of Israel for this moment. Because the Jews had been looking for the Messiah, it was necessary for them to understand Jesus was the Messiah, the one whom God had foretold. Luke did not isolate all of the passages Jesus referenced. He simply wrote that Jesus said His death and resurrection were necessary, because these had been prophesied in the Old Testament as the word of God.

Jesus focused on what was essential—His death and resurrection. You'll find any church holding to orthodox theology has affirmed the death and resurrection of Jesus Christ as true. Whether you're among the Orthodox Church of the east or Roman Catholics of the west or Protestants in these later days, there is universality of focus. Yes, it's the cross of Christ and His resurrection. The cross is God's gift for the sins of the world, and the resurrection is God's gift of hope for the world.

We have been divided about interpretations inferred by Scripture, but certain church groups don't often represent the central truth of the gospel. For some professing Christians, they would not join us at the communion table because of a difference between us. Is the difference in our belief of Christ's death for our sins? No. Is the difference in the fact that Christ was resurrected from the dead for our hope? No. So where does the difference come? It comes at the points of our understanding and interpretation. What are the important, essential beliefs?

The Council of Nicaea[10] had to deal with the question of the Trinity, for it could not have been bypassed. And when you get to Chalcedon[11] and the question of the nature of Christ, the delegates had to wrestle with that also. Who is this Christ and what is He like? Through the history of the Church universal, attempts to theologically state what we believe have become important for us. That is also the point where we draw the dividing line between people who are followers of Jesus.

Luke brought them back to Jesus' death and resurrection and basically said: "Here is the gospel, and you have a responsibility for proclaiming the truth of Christ crucified and resurrected from the dead. You are to proclaim repentance and forgiveness upon the basis of Christ."

Past experiences

Jesus pointed out the essentials in His message, but then He also recalled their experiences from the past. He said, "These are the words I've spoken to you before. You are My witnesses of these truths." To what did He refer?

First of all, they would talk about the miracles. The disciples had been present when He turned water into wine. They saw blind people receive sight; lame people who could walk; they even saw the dead raised back to life again. After the resurrection, as they undoubtedly reflected on what Christ had said to them, they also remembered what He had done. They would be His witnesses.

Jesus never went around doing miracles to entertain or impress people. Remember Satan used that temptation with Jesus: "Go up to the pinnacle of the temple and cast yourself down, and the angels of God will hold you up as the Scriptures promised. People will see and marvel. They will flock to you and say, 'Oh, this must be the Messiah.'"

In today's language Jesus said, "No way; not interested. That's not the basis for the gospel."

Sometimes we get so caught up in the miracles we forget Jesus never focused primarily on those. There are at least 35 miracles in the Gospel accounts. The writers gave no major emphasis upon them; but in truth those were a part of what the disciples witnessed.

A second observation struck me. Not only could they reflect back on the miracles they had seen, but also on His teaching. Jesus taught the truth of God in such a new way that He spoke as one with authority. He didn't speak as the rabbis who could only quote one another and base their ideas upon tradition. Jesus came and said, "Here is the significance, and here is the meaning." (See Luke 24:45–48.)

As the disciples had walked with Jesus, sat with Him around the fires at night, and traveled with Him along the dusty roads, they undoubtedly would question what He said. Before His departure from earth, Jesus said, "Remember the words I've spoken to you." His teaching was to become the basis of their proclamation.

Third, Jesus talked to them about the experience of His resurrection. How could they forget that? As they went through all those events in their minds, the biggest experience was the resurrection. Had not Jesus appeared to them? Had He not been there in the room even though the doors were locked because they feared the Jews? Didn't He suddenly appear and they saw Him?

Didn't Jesus also appear to others? Paul in his first letter to the Corinthians (chapter 15) wrote about the number of people to whom Jesus revealed Himself. When they proclaimed the gospel, one of their recollections would be: "We saw the risen Christ; we know he's alive because we've seen Him with our own eyes. Maybe that's why at the beginning of John's first letter, he wrote: "That which was from the beginning, which we have heard, which we have seen with our eyes, which we have looked at and our hands have touched — this we proclaim concerning the Word of life" (1 John 1:1).

Be His Witnesses

So between the resurrection and His ascension, Jesus told them they would be His witnesses, and those experiences had to be part of their reflections. Jesus reminded them of their responsibility to proclaim the gospel. They were to proclaim it not only to some people, but to the entire world. That was not a new thought, not for Israel. Remember Isaiah said the Jewish people were to be a light to the nations. (See Isaiah 49:6.) You can go through the Old Testament and document the fact that God's will was never an isolated blessing to a single group of people. In the beginning with Abraham, God said that in the seed of

Abraham all of the nations would be blessed. (See Genesis 18:18 and Galatians 3:8.) When Isaiah said the Israelites were to be a light to the nations, it wasn't anything brand new.

Through the years, the Jewish people began to pull in their perimeters until they circled their wagons around their own little group of people and they treated it as: "This is our blessing. This is our truth, and the only way you can know this truth is to become a part of us." They isolated themselves in many different ways, and that hasn't stopped over the centuries.

Today Jesus sends us to proclaim His gospel, and we're to proclaim it to the entire world. He laid a burden upon the disciples' hearts and it's to continue with us. I am staggered with the imagination of that kind of task being laid upon them and upon us.

Now, that leads me to observe a fourth point. Jesus also brought the disciples face to face to deal with their doubts. From the beginning, when the women reported they had seen and heard Jesus, some disciples doubted it. It's reported there were among them those who did not believe. Why not? What an amazing thought! He was dead; they had laid His body in a tomb. They knew He was dead, and now others said He was alive. They doubted it then, but by this time they had seen Him enough to know He was alive. Through those forty days, Jesus eased their doubts and brought them to the place where with a positive affirmation they could say, "Jesus is not dead. He is alive, and we have seen Him."

I have to wonder, though, if their doubts were in a great part about themselves. Jesus told them to go and proclaim the gospel to all of the nations. If I had been there that day I would want to respond like this, "Who me?" Look at those guys. They had all forsaken Him and fled. Peter had denied Him three different times. Now Jesus was saying to those who had demonstrated their own weakness that the task would be theirs. They were to go into the world—all of the world—and tell what God had done through His gift of the Messiah. They struggled with doubts, and it's at this point Jesus gave them three answers.

Promise of His Presence

First of all, Jesus had already given them His presence. He had been with them and appeared to them in a number of different places. They had seen and heard him; they had touched him. They knew He is a risen man, not an apparition, not a figment of their spiritual imaginations. No, He was flesh and bones. His was a bodily resurrection. Also, He promised He would always be with them. Matthew added at the end of his Gospel: "And surely I am with you always, to the very end of the age" (28:20).

When Jesus gave the disciples their task, I don't know what kind of murmuring must have gone on, but they probably began to look at each other and shaking their heads, asked: "Lord how can we do this? Who are *we* to carry this message? You know our failures, and we're uneducated men. People don't even recognize us as leaders of the community."

Jesus again reminded them: "I'm not leaving you to the task by yourself. I am with you."

When we celebrate Eucharist, Communion, the Lord's Supper (all the names we give it), it's a reminder not only of what Jesus did but the promise of His presence. The Church through the centuries has understood, somehow or another, that in the broken bread and the cup, there is the presence of Christ himself. Some have said the elements themselves have transformed. Others say no, it's not transformed but enveloped in the sense of Christ's presence. However people understand that at the table is the presence of the Lord. That's why we can account for the table becoming such a vital part of church worship. Jesus meets with us around His table.

Jesus gave them His presence, but He also gave them the promise God had already made. Joel prophesied: "I will pour out my Spirit upon all people. Your sons and daughters will prophesy, your old men will dream dreams, your young men will see visions" (2:28). Jesus affirmed that promise of the Father would be fulfilled. Jesus had given them a great task, but they would not do it in their own strength. The Holy Spirit would be present with them, the *Paracletos*, the one who stands alongside.

The Holy Spirit is the one who comforts in the sense of strengthening, but He is also the one who stands as the Advocate for us. So Jesus said to the disciples: "On my account you will be brought before governors and kings as witnesses to them and to the Gentiles. But when they arrest you, do not worry about what to say or how to say it. At that time you will be given what to say, for it will not be you speaking, but the Spirit of your Father speaking through you" (Matthew 10:18–20). The Advocate was there with them and is here with us.

The Holy Spirit is not only the Advocate, but also a teacher. Well, I don't know how they felt, but I've studied the Bible for many years and I'm still ignorant of this book. It contains much more I need to learn. It's one of the greatest regrets as I've gotten older; there's so little time to grasp all of what I want to know. Jesus said, "Look, I'm not going to leave you. The Holy Spirit will be there and He's going to be your teacher."

I'm sure many of them were thinking, *But Lord, what about when we get into various, troubling kinds of situations?*

Jesus essentially said, "Remember the Holy Spirit will be your guide. When it comes to the matter of choices, decisions to be made; when it comes to a matter of confronting life itself, I'm giving you an unerring guide; for He knows the truth and will teach you the truth." (See John 16:13.)

Promise of Power

What Jesus did last was to promise them power. Now, we human beings don't deal well with power. Sad to say, we in the ministry don't always deal well with power. We tend to say that absolute power corrupts absolutely, and power is not good for us, because we're tempted to abuse and misuse it. Too many times through the history of the church, we can point to instances and say, "Yes, here is a case where power was abused." Nonetheless, Jesus promised the disciples power.

Jesus said they would be *clothed* with power. That imagery jumps out to me. Clothing provides a covering for our nakedness; and in the same sense Jesus said there's a power that will be like clothing and it's going to be sufficient, adequate. No matter how naked we may be in our weakness, we will be given the power of God to clothe us for whatever circumstances we face. Our own weaknesses will be covered and not apparent, because the power of God will be working in us.

Jesus made one other pronouncement, the one most interesting for me. In our Bible it says: "I am going to send you what my Father has promised; but stay in the city until you have been clothed with power from on high" (Luke 24:49). It's a common observation, but "from on high" means divine, supernatural power. What Jesus promised those men was the power they had seen operating in Him; that same power would be present to operate within their lives. I don't know how they handled that. I don't know how you or I handle that. It's daunting to understand the idea that, somehow or other, God is going to place within the hands of those disciples, people like you and me, such a supernatural power that's capable of being used for the sake of the kingdom of God.

Note Jesus inserted, "But stay in the city until..." (Luke 24:49). It's translated different ways. Some versions take it as: Don't leave Jerusalem until you've been endued with power from on high. The Greek word there means "sit down." How fascinating! He'd given them all those promises and when He got to the end, He said, "Now sit down." Jesus told them to wait, that's for sure.

He said not to leave Jerusalem until something extraordinary happened.

The waiting time was necessary before the disciples launched out in this ministry of the church. "When they arrived, they went upstairs to the rooms where they were staying.... They all joined together constantly in prayer" (Acts 1:13,14).

Here I want to make a direct application to us. First was the necessity of integrating everything that had gone on for three and a half years—all they felt, all they saw and heard. They would integrate that into some kind of wholeness, if you please, some kind of witness they could put their hands around, their minds around. That may seem rather idle to you, but I don't think it is. The necessity of integrating the gospel message, understanding it clearly so when they went out to speak, it's not as one grasping for the truth but knowing what's in their hands. They took time; they needed time to integrate.

Second, they needed the time to get beyond some of their petty rivalries. You remember on the way to Jerusalem they argued among themselves: Who is going to sit at the right hand of Jesus and who's going to sit at the left?

I heard an evangelist many years ago preaching on the ten days the apostles were in the upper room with others, praying before the Holy Spirit fell on the church. This evangelist stated it took ten days of praying to work out all that had divided them. I don't have any trouble believing that. In most churches it'd probably take longer than ten days. The disciples needed to set aside their petty jealousies, puny rivalries, the desire to be number one, or at least to be in the places of recognition and authority.

Let me put this another way. They needed time to die to themselves. That's a tall order. To die in terms of their relationships with one another, also to die to themselves literally in the sense of taking up the gospel message to proclaim it. "Had not the Master said we must take up our crosses and follow him, and not to do so meant we could not be His disciples? Jesus said we need to understand the cost involved and what's demanded. It may mean our lives."

I suggest they had to get to the place where they recognized the price of discipleship and to say, "Yes, Lord, all the way, even to the cross." Everything Jesus said to them underscored that. They needed time to pray, didn't they?

Let's come back and look at this from the standpoint of you and me today.

If Jesus spoke to us today, He would say, "You are my witnesses."

Would it not be true that we have seen the risen Christ? Oh, we didn't sit in a closed room with the doors locked and see Him physically appear before us. But we are His witnesses.

I don't know when you saw Jesus, but we have all had opportunities. Some of us may say: "Yes, I remember. It was one day when I felt the bottom of my life had collapsed. I thought everything was lost. Somehow I sensed His presence."

Have we not seen Jesus in the love and wisdom of our mothers and in fathers? Have we not seen Him in the laughter of our children? Have we not seen Him beside an open grave even while tears coursed down our cheeks? Didn't we sense Jesus along the road where we came to our own resistance and He met us there as He met Paul on the road to Damascus.

Even in the face of our recalcitrance, He dared reveal Himself, and we knew He was with us. Wasn't it in that moment when we felt we had failed so terribly and Jesus met us? He reminded us we belong to Him. He has forgiven us, and even in our failure we know the sense of His presence. Wasn't it in the beauty of nature when somehow we had an overwhelming sense of not being alone? Well, if we haven't sensed Him in any of those experiences, then we have no gospel to proclaim, and Jesus becomes only a figure in literature. But if we have known Him, then we are His witnesses.

When have I seen Jesus? Jesus has come to me in those deepest, darkest hours. He has met me in the most beautiful days of life. He has been beside me time and time again, even when I didn't sense His presence. I am His witness. We are His witnesses.

Proclaim the Gospel

We *all* need to proclaim His gospel. That's not the sole responsibility of the paid ministry. When I look at the business of ordained clergy, I find nothing in the New Testament that indicates there was an extraordinary, supernatural ordination. There were certainly positions of leadership, elders and deacons, and the church appointed them for various tasks. But at no place do I find such a division created so that some of us have a responsibility and the rest of us are along for the ride. That isn't the way it works. We are all called to be witnesses, and that means we're called to proclaim the gospel. It's your task as well as mine.

The world needs the message of Christ's life, death, and resurrection, but the message is not going to come only by what is spoken from pulpits. Pastors are given the job of training people in the faith, strengthening them to become whole persons. But each person goes out into the business place and neighborhood, meeting with friends, saying, "Let me tell you about Jesus Christ and what He has done for me."

Oh, you say, "I'm not a Bible scholar. I haven't been to seminary." May I give you an interesting fact? Most people don't care. They know little about theology or philosophy. But they do know when a life has been transformed, when a life is brought in an integrated wholeness with the gospel of peace and love, when people love others not because there's something in it for them, but because they are related to the One who loves the world.

That's what the world is waiting to hear, waiting to see, and that's your job and mine as we're in our communities and with our families. We bring the truth of the gospel of Jesus Christ and we integrate the kingdom of God into our lives so what we do and what we think and how we respond to circumstances and situations reflect how we proclaim and live the gospel. Sometimes it's necessary to speak, but oftentimes that isn't the key. It is the fact that we live it. One of the last things Jesus said to the early church and to us was, "Sit down."

I hesitated to include that point, because in a lot of churches that's exactly where people are, where a lot of them have been for a long time. And I don't want that image to come across as static. We're not talking about sitting down and doing nothing, but what Jesus said to those disciples was, "I want you to come apart and sit down; wait and pray."

I suggest there's nothing more important for us who name the name of Christ than to find the place where we can sit down and be quiet. We need it on a daily basis, because we need daily to reflect on our relationship with Christ and His relationship with us. If we don't take time to be quiet, we end up with lives that are never examined, and consequently we often get away from the base line. We need time to integrate Christ's teaching. We need time to reflect on Jesus. We need time to come to the place where we understand what Jesus is saying to us: "Whoever wants to be my disciples must deny themselves and take up their cross and follow me" (Matthew 16:24).

I had a pastor stop by the house one day and he talked about wanting to do something within his church. So he had a board meeting. "I stood up and started the meeting this way," he said. "I asked one question: I know we're all busy people, but how many of you are willing to give one more hour out of your week for the sake of something we need to do in the church?" He said nobody responded. He told me, "I looked at them and said: Meeting is over. Let's go home." That puts the finger on one of the problems we have as Christians. Would we give one more hour for

Jesus who gave His life for us upon a cross? One more hour?

How do we draw lines and limits? At what place can I stand in front of the Lord of creation and say, this far and no farther? At what place can I ask Him who gave Himself for me: "I'm not willing to go that far for You"? If you have trouble with that question, moms and dads, where do you draw the line for your children? Would you ever say, I only love you this far and no farther?

We need time, time to come to the place where we're ready to take up our cross and follow Jesus, and we need time to pray because until we find that time we'll never find the answer to anything else.

At the end of Luke's Gospel, we see the church was about to be birthed. It was about to break loose in the world. Those disciples had a horrendously difficult task, and Jesus said, "Come aside. Take time out."

So would you take a few moments to ask what the Lord is saying to you out of this passage of Scripture? You heard what Jesus said to the disciples. Ask Jesus now, "What are You saying to Me?"

Prayer: Jesus, You gave the disciples Your presence, a promise always to be with them. You gave them the power of the Holy Spirit to enable them to proclaim the gospel of salvation to the whole world. But You did not stop there. You have given each one of us in this day and age those same gifts: Your presence and the power of the Holy Spirit. What are You saying to us who are Your present-day followers? As we think of family members, friends, and co-workers who need You, we ask for Your power to speak Your word boldly. We know You will be with us. In Your holy name we ask. Amen.

CHAPTER THREE

The Church as the Body of Christ

Part A: The Body Taking Shape
Acts 2:41–47

"He is the head of the body, the church; he is the beginning and the firstborn from among the dead, so that in everything he might have the supremacy." —Colossians 1:18

We come to the second chapter of Acts and begin with verse forty-one and close with verse forty-seven.

Those who accepted his [Peter's] message were baptized, and about three thousand were added to their number that day. They devoted themselves to the apostles' teaching and to fellowship, to the breaking of bread and to prayer. Everyone was filled with awe at the many wonders and signs performed by the apostles. All the believers were together and had everything in common. They sold property and possessions to give to anyone who had need. Every day they continued to meet together in the temple courts. They broke bread in their homes and ate together with glad and sincere hearts, praising God and enjoying the favor of all the people. And the Lord added to their number daily those who were being saved. —Acts 2:41–47

For each of us, life began not with our actual birth into the world, but with our conception. I never thought much about that, but my mother-in-law used to remind us she was older than the age we celebrated on her birthday. Nine months to be exact. All of us had that kind of beginning.

As we look at the church, we find a parallel. As our bodies took shape in the womb of our mothers, so the church began to take shape in the womb of Jerusalem. It became the church as we later came to know it. We often celebrate Pentecost as though that were the day the church materialized. However, that was only the beginning of the beginning, for in Jerusalem the church began to take shape.

If we're to understand what the church should be today, then we need to understand what it was, how it started. We can't divorce ourselves from the beginning of the church, its initial formation and what God intended it to be in those early stages. For any group of people, organization, or the body of Christ, to lose sight of its heritage is to lose its identity. The church maintains its identity by being what God raised it up to be in the beginning.

If you'll pardon this kind of imagery, the church, like children, derives certain characteristics from father and mother. Now before you get too shook up over that statement, let me explain. Obviously when we go back to the book of Acts and look at the beginning of the church becoming the body of Christ, we know it received gifts from the Father. We definitely recognize the gift of the Son—the message of redemption, incorporated into the existence of the body of Christ.

As we read in the second chapter of Acts, the gift of the Holy Spirit was also evident. God poured out His Spirit upon the early church. To identify the character of the church in the first century, we can't omit either the gifts of the Father, Christ the redeemer, and the indwelling of the Holy Spirit.

Begin in the Old Testament

We tend, however, to forget that the church had a mother. I'm not going to push this imagery too far, but the church didn't come into existence out of nothing. When you go back into the old covenant, there's the formation of what became the church in the New Testament. So we would be in error if we think the church of the New Testament is totally different from the church of the Old Testament. I'm not insisting on this imagery of the church having a mother in any literal sense, but as the church derived gifts from the Father, it also derived much of what existed in the Old Testament covenant. We must never forget that the church didn't suddenly appear as though it had no relationship with what had existed before.

Between the old and the new covenants there's no break, but a fulfillment of the old covenant in the new. The church does not exist apart from what it inherited from the old covenant. Now you say, "What are you talking about exactly?" For example, take the language used. You say, the New Testament is Greek, and the Old Testament is Hebrew. I'm going deeper than that. Let's take what words are used: justify and sanctify. Those terms go back to the Old Testament. In reading the Old Testament you can better understand the meaning of those terms as they're used in the New Testament. I'm not suggesting the words didn't take on additional nuances in the New Testament, but certainly they were established in the Old Testament.

The vocabulary of the New Testament has to be interpreted in terms of the Hebrew Old Testament. Theologically, the Old Testament gave birth to those meanings. So when Paul starts describing what he believes theologically, he takes it right out of the old covenant. True, the covenant is fulfilled, but it's not eradicated. That's why we have an Old Testament as well as a New Testament.

As a young man right out of college, I accepted my first supply pastorate in Biloxi, Mississippi. I bought a car from a Christian man, and while we were driving around he talked about church, knowing I was a pastor. He made this statement: "Well, I belong to a New Testament church." I didn't know what he meant, but now I know he's dead wrong. There isn't any such thing as a New Testament church, because the heritage of the New Testament comes out of the Old Testament. The fulfillment in the New is what God had begun in the Old. To forget that is to fall into the error of insisting the God of the New Testament is different than the God of the Old Testament. That's foolish. The God of the New Testament is the same in the Old Testament as He unfolds His plan of redemption.

Some say the Old Testament is law and the New Testament is grace, and I believe that's totally false. To say there's no grace in the Old Testament is to close our eyes. Anybody named Hannah? Rejoice! Your name comes from the Hebrew word *chann*, which means grace and mercy. God is a gracious God.

To say the New Testament doesn't include law is also to close our eyes. One example would be the Sermon on the Mount where Jesus said clearly, "Do not think that I have come to abolish the Law or the Prophets; I have not come to abolish them but to fulfill them" (Matthew 5:17).

Murder and adultery and covetousness are no more accepted in the New Testament than in the Old, because the Old Testament Law was the moral photograph of God and fulfilled in the New Testament. The church took shape from its mother Judaism. That's true whether we're talking about ethics or language or theology, or whether we're talking about worship. It might surprise you to know that the basic structure of Christian worship came directly out of the synagogue.

Yes, you can compare the two services and they follow right along. Why? Because people establishing the early church were Jews. They didn't consider themselves non-Jews because they were now Christians. What does a Messianic Jew call himself now? A completed Jew. We can't forget that, because as we look at the book of Acts and the formation of the church, we have to remember the church didn't drop out of heaven as something that never had any previous existence. It is the fulfillment of what God had already started.

The early believers shaped the church. We notice they continued steadfastly in their various aspects of church worship. There we find the foundations being laid for the church today, not separate and distinct from the church as it was in its beginning.

When we look at this passage in the second chapter of Acts, we notice the people accepted Peter's words. That is, they believed his words were true and responded by being baptized. They committed themselves to Christ as they confessed Christ as the Messiah. They joined themselves with Peter, James, John, Matthew, the rest of the disciples, the rest of the one hundred twenty persons who had been in the upper room praying and waiting for the coming of the Holy Spirit, as well as many others who were not present at that particular time.

Devoted Practices

Luke said they continued steadfastly, which to me means they were focused entirely upon several practices. He listed four of them and you've heard them before, but I call your attention to them, because it's important for us in our day.

First, "They devoted themselves to the apostles' teaching" (Acts 2:42). These men had spent years with Jesus, three years perhaps. They had listened to His teachings, and now it was imperative for those early Christians to understand the truth Christ had taught. It is also imperative for us to know what we believe. We cannot believe what we don't know. That's why I've said repeatedly—to separate your heart from your head is nonsense.

I hear people say that a person is a Christian in the head but it hasn't reached the heart yet. In other words, with their minds they're totally convinced, but it hasn't affected their hearts. I ask, "How could their hearts be in any kind of personal relationship with Christ unless they know who He is." The mind and heart work together, part and parcel of what it means to have faith. After Peter preached on the day of Pentecost, and the people responded, Peter wanted to begin to meet together and know what Jesus taught.

Scholars believe there began at this point a collection of the sayings of Jesus. They called it the Q document. The Source Q is an undocumented or unknown source which contains differences in the synoptic Gospels. When they wrote the gospel accounts they borrowed rather substantially from those sayings in the life of the early church. This is important, because the word in Greek (*paradosis*) means "surrender" or "giving over by word of mouth or writing." From this we get the idea of tradition. Sometimes the word is viewed as rather negative. We feel traditions bind us to the past and are obsolete and no longer valuable. But I remind you in order to understand what the church should be, we have to understand how it came into existence. What was its purpose? What was its heart? We agree traditions are important, and we are fools if we lose our traditions. That doesn't mean every tradition is good. Some traditions ought to be lost, but some have to be kept, for they maintain our identity, who we are.

I once had the privilege of sitting with a friend and her sister as they began to reminisce about their family. I found out about their particular traditions. We all have our family traditions. In fact, I suspect that many of our practices today have been determined by what we grew up doing. Those traditions are meaningful to us. So it is with the church.

We don't sanctify tradition. We don't lift tradition up as though we bow before something holy. But we cannot lose who we are; for if we do, we don't know where we're going or what we should be.

The early church learned the teachings of the apostles. The second thing we notice is they gave themselves to community, the *koinonia*. Now we have to put the definite article in there, because it wasn't simply the word for fellowship. In other words, they got together for *the* fellowship. Now you say, "What do you mean by that?" I think the Bible points out the strength of community lay not only in the fact that they got together and ate, but they were building the body of Christ, the fellowship for Christians. They were not simply having a good time visiting with one another, they understood this was a specialized community. We call it the family of God.

That's different from other kinds of fellowships. For example, you and I have friends who are not Christians. Perhaps they belong to other religions, but we enjoy being with them. We meet for a time of eating, laughing, and having fun. But there is something about the Christian family that stands distinctive to those kinds of relationships. This is why it is so important for the church to be in community.

Given our present tendencies today, it's sad when we see each other only on Sundays and hardly know one another. At times people have come to me and asked, "Do you know who Joe Blow is? I don't know him." It's evident we don't know people who are in the fellowship of our church. We have lost the sense of being bound together in a special way. The meaning of the word *koinonia* provides that common center which brings us into a relationship with one another. As we confess Jesus Christ as Lord and Savior, that commitment to His lordship binds us together as fellow believers.

The early church concerned themselves with the fellowship. We notice also they had a sense of exclusivity. It's a sense in which others are not a part. A special relationship exists between Christians. As I've travelled in many different countries I've discovered how true that is. I can be with people who speak other languages, who look quite differently than I do, dress in varied styles, and have unique customs. Their whole ethnicity may be totally different, and yet there is something that binds us together in the fellowship of the saints.

Celebrating Communion

Then you notice thirdly, they joined in the breaking of bread and again the definite article is important: *the* breaking of bread. The reference here is clearly the idea of celebrating the Lord's Supper or the Eucharist or the communion service, whatever we want to call it. They met and broke the bread together. As for us today, it is the necessity of rehearsal.

Caution: the Lord's Table can become common place. I visited a church in California where they serve communion ever Sunday. While we received the plates with elements for communion, other things were going on at the same time—they also passed offering plates and a soloist sang. In fact, the two pastors sat on the platform talking to one another. I wondered: *Is this a tradition we do automatically and don't know its full significance?*

When the early church met, they broke the bread together and they had that sense of rehearsal, for in biblical theology we have the idea of recital. We find it in the Old Testament where there is recital of events that refresh, renew, and remind us of what life is. Sharing communion should remind us we are bought with a price. Christ suffered for my sins. He bore my sins and carried my sorrows. How can I take the broken bread; how can I take the cup and not remember Him? So, they gave themselves to the breaking of the bread.

I may differ from a lot of people, but I think one of the tragedies in the church today is (for want of a better term) we have sacramentalized some practices. Now you say: What do you mean by that? I don't mean it's not a sacrament. We have two sacraments in the Protestant church—both of which were commanded by our Lord. Jesus said, "Do this." Baptism and the Lord's Supper we take as sacraments. But we've done something the early church did not do. We took the breaking of the bread out of the home, out of the common experiences we share with one another, and we make it a sacred ritual only done in the church; and the elements have to be consecrated by a fully ordained clergy person. In the book of Acts we do not find fully ordained clergy.

Where did we get the idea that only clergy can break bread and remember Christ's sacrifice? I think the reason Jesus took the bread and the wine is He used two common elements in their lives, so every time they sat at table and broke bread and drank wine with their meal, they could remember Christ and rehearse Him. Now that doesn't mean we do away with it in our worship services, but it could mean we've elevated communion into some kind of great position that makes most of us feel like it's not common anymore. They gathered in homes and broke the bread together.

The fourth practice is they gathered for the prayers. They were continuing steadfastly in the prayers. What does that mean? If Luke had simply said, they gathered together to pray, we would say: Yeah, they got together and prayed. But they gathered together for *the* prayers. I suggest the prayers included many of the Old Testament prayers that had become a part of the Jewish tradition. If you visit a synagogue today, you discover they recite the prayers used for centuries. Those were their formalized prayers, similar to what we read sometimes in church today, such as in the confession of sins.

You may say: I don't believe in reading written prayers. In Wesley's day those were the only prayers they did believe in using. It was almost heresy to pray extemporaneously. Those formal prayers are valuable, because so often they are collections of what we often forget. I don't know if you listen to pastoral prayers. As I go from one church to another, I've heard prayers with the same words being used and it's as if we're locked in to certain things we pray about. In the early church I don't think they ever separated formal prayers in their worship services from the prayers they prayed extemporaneously. That's true for us today.

I've spent time reading books of prayers, and it's not boring. It's one of the most spiritually enlightening and beneficial practices I've done. Often I find in the words of others beautiful expressions in their prayers that help me know how to pray. I recommend it.

To Establish Unity

The early church gathered together in the four foundational aspects of community: the teaching of the apostles, the fellowship, the breaking of the bread, and the prayers. As they met together to establish unity, they formed and fashioned the fellowship that became so important to the church. In other words, they were not separate Christians drifting apart from one another. They shared a common center, rejoicing in what Christ had done for them. They prayed together for what God was doing in their personal lives, but also for the concerns of the local community. I dare say, as they gathered in fellowship, again and again they rejoiced in the centrality of Jesus as Savior and Lord, and they rejoiced in the common experience they shared—redemption and belonging to a kingdom not of this world.

The church today finds its meaning by learning from the early church. We cannot be what we ought to be unless we understand what first we were. As we begin to work on this, we come together "praising God and enjoying the favor of all the people" (Acts 2:47).

The early church gathered in the love of Christ and for one another. (See 2 Thessalonians 1:3.) One of the most striking points in the passage in Acts is how these people had such selfless respect for those who gathered with them. Notice how and why they came together. As they saw each other's needs, they reached out to help. We know people in Israel in those days were not wealthy.

Compared to much of the rest of the world, they experienced poverty. Later we find Paul took collections for the church in Jerusalem, and that seemed to be part of the early church's concern. (See 1 Corinthians 16:1–3.) They shared freely of themselves with one another.

Notice what Luke wrote: They sold their possessions and personal belongings and distributed the proceeds to anyone who had need (Acts 2:45). I've heard people say, "That's Communism." I'm not suggesting for a moment this statement is a policy for the development of government and politics. What I am saying is, as Christians, we can never enjoy the blessings of life while others do not know those blessings. Over the years I've noticed the church's concern for one another. When a need exists in someone's life, the response in many a congregation turns out as: "I want to help. What can I do?" Sometimes it's a matter of financial help. Sometimes it's being physically present for someone. Again and again the church meets a need.

Those early Christians came together, sharing in one another's needs. They broke the bread together; they enjoyed the fellowship together. Because they loved each other, they found a common meal as a wonderful way to gather.

Some church folk view eating in church as next door to heresy. That's too bad, because we've forgotten the early church took great joy in times they shared a meal together. Some of the greatest times I've discovered in church fellowship has not been found when we're sitting like wooden statues in pews but rather when we have time to relax and be with one another in breaking of bread, in sharing of ourselves, in getting to know one another. During Sunday worship we could find wonderful stories in everyone we meet. We don't know them because we don't take time together. If there's any strong argument against having large churches, it begins here. When we do not know each other, we miss the blessings of Christ others have experienced.

So we look at those people who from the beginning were poor, and later economic sanctions would be levied against them. Read about some of their hardships in chapters ten and twelve of Hebrews. The writer wrote about the financial suffering through which they had passed. Then he said: "Hang in there and be strong, you have not yet suffered to the shedding of blood." They worshipped together, sang together, prayed together, and bonded together, because they blessed God as one community.

Starting a Church Today

Two questions: First, what would we do if we were starting up a church in our day? I find that to be a refreshing and wonderful idea. If we were starting from scratch now, what would we do? Think of the various concepts that would be vital and necessary. Before we say much, we need to go back to Acts chapter two and see what the early church looked like. How do we implement those principles in the church today?

Of course, that's not to say there would not be changes to make. The church has been fluid through 2000 years. It has never been a stagnant, unmoving body of believers. The church through the centuries has always been adjusting and adapting in the same way that was true even in the Old Testament. Yes, we do recognize what could to be done differently. But we ought to know why and how these relate to who we are and what is our purpose.

To forget that part is to be victimized by the contemporary society around us. Too many Christians and churches are being molded by a secular culture. We don't need to be like the world. But neither do we need to be odd balls.

The church changes. But for what reason does it change? We go back to Acts to see what it was that made them effective and dynamic. As long as we maintain the centrality of Christ we see in the early church, then we can be the church that's needed for this generation. It may be a different kind of church, but at the same time the best church for the twenty-first century.

So the last question is: What do we do about this? We go back and see this picture of the early church and how they took shape, the foundational elements. Once the foundation has been laid, we can build on it all of the various services that are needed. Without the foundation, no matter what we build, it will not stand the tests of time.

Take a moment to reflect about the early church and ask yourself some questions. How should the church be shaped today? Remember our heritage: what the church was in its beginning and who we are now. How can we be that and at the same time minister to the world in which we live today?

Prayer: Lord Jesus, we desire to follow You in our day and age. Help us to stand on the firm foundation of the centrality of who You are and then who You want us to be—as individuals who make up the church locally and at large. Give us Your wisdom and the power of the Holy Spirit to shape the church of today, meeting the needs of today. In Your name we pray. Amen.

CHAPTER FOUR

The Church as the Body of Christ

Part B: The Body of Christ
Ephesians 4:1–16

"His intent was that now, through the church, the manifold wisdom of God should be made known to the rulers and authorities in the heavenly realms, according to his eternal purpose that he accomplished in Christ Jesus our Lord." —Ephesians 3:10–11

For this subject on the church I go to the book of Ephesians. We look at the fourth chapter of Ephesians. This is a beautiful passage of Scripture. We begin with verse one and read through the sixteenth verse.

As a prisoner for the Lord, then, I urge you to live a life worthy of the calling you have received. Be completely humble and gentle; be patient, bearing with one another in love. Make every effort to keep the unity of the Spirit through the bond of peace. There is one body and one Spirit, just as you were called to one hope when you were called; one Lord, one faith, one baptism; one God and Father of all, who is over all and through all and in all. But to each one of us grace has been given as Christ apportioned it. This why it says: "When he ascended on high, he took many captives and gave gifts to his people." [Psalm 68:18] (What does "he ascended" mean except that he also descended to the lower, earthly regions? He who descended is the very one who ascended higher than all the heavens, in order to fill the whole universe.) So Christ himself gave the apostles, the prophets, the evangelists, the pastors and teachers, to equip his people for works of service, so that the body of Christ may be built up until we all reach unity in the faith and in the knowledge of the Son of God and become mature, attaining to the whole measure of the fullness of Christ. Then we will no longer be infants, tossed back and forth by the waves, and blown here and there by every wind of teaching and by the cunning and craftiness of people in their deceitful scheming. Instead, speaking the truth in love, we will grow to become in every respect the mature body of him who is the head, that is, Christ. From him the whole body, joined and held

*together by every supporting ligament, grows and
builds itself up in love, as each part does its work.*
—Ephesians 4:1–16

I would personally list Paul's letter to the
Ephesians as his second greatest letter. Obviously
Romans gets first place in everybody's book, but
Ephesians is a marvelous book. Unlike other letters Paul wrote, he was not addressing a specific
church. In fact, the little phrase "in Ephesus" at
the beginning of this letter is not in the oldest
manuscripts. Perhaps it came to be associated
with Ephesus, because that was the major church
in the area of Asia Minor.

In the book of Revelation, where John wrote
about the seven churches, he began with Ephesus
and circles around. As we read the book of
Ephesians, we discover not a particular group
but the church at large. In this letter Paul sees the
church in a universal sense. His vision was not
only for local churches or local bodies of Christ,
but for the body of Christ universal, not as a single entity.

In the first three chapters Paul wrote about the
basis of the church itself. It is founded upon what
God has done for us in Christ. God has given us
every spiritual blessing in the heavenly places in
Christ according as He has chosen us—that's the

way Paul begins the letter. He wrote that the body of believers is The Church, not simply an individual church. Through three chapters he wrote about what God wants to do in the lives of those who have come to faith in Jesus Christ. Paul ended the third chapter with a beautiful doxology: "Now to him who is able to do immeasurably more than all we ask or imagine, according to the power that is at work within us, to him be glory in the church and in Christ Jesus throughout all generations, for ever and ever! Amen" (vv. 20–21).

Paul then made a transition, a pivotal point. Having addressed the church basically in terms of what it is and what their faith is, how God has worked in the lives of these people, he then began to make the application to individual lives, our personal living within communities. When I first started reading Ephesians, I understood clearly that our Christianity is not simply in the pronunciation of our faith (our creedal statements) but faith is the way we live before the constituency around us—our family, neighbors, and fellow citizens.

Beginning in this fourth chapter, Paul urged them to walk worthy of the high calling with which they've been called. You notice in this letter he used the word "walk" a number of times (about seven or eight times), and this little word depicts in Paul's mind not only the fact that we believe something, but we live something. In the NIV translation and most of our versions today, it's stated as "live a life worthy of the calling" (v. 1). Paul's use of the word *walk* creates a beautiful image. It's how we walk, how we live. We talk about that all the time—you have to walk the walk as well as talk the talk. So Paul long ago talked about how we *used to* walk: We walked in our sins, transgressions, and old habits. We were in darkness at that time, but then he wrote about our walk as Christians.

Intensity Due to Choices

In the word "then" (4:1), Paul pivoted from what he'd been saying to ask: "How do we live this?" And he didn't write in an individual sense, although it implies individual lives. He talked to the body of Christ, addressing the congregation of believers. Not one community, but wherever the letter would be read. "I urge you to live a life worthy of the calling you have received" (4:1).

To read that intense statement we know what Paul has said here is not: "Hey, this is a good idea, you ought to practice this." The NIV translates it: "I urge you." But I prefer the word "beg," because that's everyday English to us: "I beg you to do this." So here Paul called them to remember what they believe, and that their walk is totally different from their walk when they did not know Christ.

If I came to you and said, "I beg you to do this," then you recognize a bit of intensity in my request. So Paul is intense in what we all must realize. Our hands are on the tiller of the ship of faith on which we live. On your individual boat, you're the one guiding. The boat is going in the direction you intend.

Paul's intensity here is, in part, to recognize people who have been created by God are free to make needed choices as Christians. God doesn't compel us. I am not a determinist by any stretch of the imagination. If determinism were true, there would be no such thing as virtue. If there's no choice, because I'm compelled to do something, then there's no virtue in doing it. Right? It's like having broken your leg. You have to walk on crutches, and there's no virtue in that. You don't have any choice. What I read Paul begging the people reminds me again that God has created us in His image, and part of that image is the free will He has placed within us.

I read an article in which the writer stated that unlike Augustine, who was revered by Luther, Calvin, and Zwingli, the evangelical church today is more Pelagian.[12] I won't get into the theology, but it's about the difference between freedom of the will and the idea that you and I are elected to be Christians. It's not a decision we make; we are chosen and God's grace is irresistible. I'm not going to structure my ideas on Augustine, Luther, Calvin, Zwingli, and Wesley; they're not our textbook. Our textbook is the Bible, and I hear Paul saying, "People, I beg you to do this." So it's not an automatic thing; it is something we have the choice of doing.

You and I choose how we're going to live. You're not predestined to live one way or another. Each of us makes that choice. Every time you come to a choice in your life, you're going to make a decision. Paul intensely urged these people to come to the place where they make choices to live according to the calling they've received.

Urgency Due to Culture

To "walk worthy" is not only intention, it's urgent, because Paul knew the pressures around us are exceedingly strong. Do any of us need to be reminded of that today? In America the church in large measure is often being dictated by the culture, rather than the church dictating to the culture. Falling in line, too often we want to identify with the culture. We can move so far in that direction until we can't tell the difference between the church and those outside the church. Don't forget: Christianity grew up in the circle of pagan religions. No Christian countries existed at that time.

The church and individuals within the church had to battle their way through the environment around them. They had to be strong then and we still have to now. Paul begged the people, because he knew very well that the culture's pressures can be so persistent and invasive they easily override our principles.

We experience that today, don't we? People spout their beliefs, and yet when they act contrary ways, we stop and ask: "Why did they do that?" The world will override us unless our principles are stronger than the pressures around us. That's what Paul said: "I beg you to walk worthy of your high calling." The model has been set for us. We see in Christ the principles by which we ought to be living; so Paul said, let's get out there and live it. Remember, he's writing to Christians, not unbelievers. He's writing to church people, the body of Christ, so he said: "I beg you to follow Christ's example." (See Ephesians 4:15.)

Paul knew, as we must realize, that our choices inform the conclusions we draw. Choices inform consequences. When you say, "I don't know why that happened," back up and look at the choices you made, and you'll know exactly why it happened. Our choices lead us to particular consequences. It's true for all of our lives, so Paul begged them with intensity and with urgency about how they need to walk.

Paul also emphasized that *unity* is needed in the church. Let's look at two different factors he stated that make unity possible.

Personal Virtues

First, Paul wrote about personal virtues that are important if the church is going to be the church. Reading through this passage, I thought of an article I'd clipped out in May of 2000. In "Forget Values, Let's Talk Virtues," George F. Will[13] wrote about the necessity of personal virtues. Here's what he wrote: "When you hear . . . politicians speaking of 'values,' you are in the presence of America's problem, not its solution." He goes on to set the stage: "Values are an equal-opportunity business: They are mere choices. Virtues are habits, difficult to develop and therefore not equally accessible to all." What is Will driving at? Let's stop and think about it.

In any church or organization, if we asked about values, people would list all kinds of values. Many would be the same, but some values would not be the same as others. For example, someone would stand up and say, "I value the time when I go play golf every week." Others would say, "Oh, good luck; we're not faintly interested in playing golf." George Will explained that when you stop and think about values, those will differ from group to group or person to person because they are choices.

My values may not be your values. Your values may not be somebody else's values. In fact, your values may differ from a person who's related to you. Values, George Will said, are choices we make; but virtues are habits, principles by which life is shaped. Will was driving home about how we talk about values all the time, but we don't talk much about virtues. In Paul's letter, he wrote about four virtues: humility, gentleness, patience, and tolerance.

Humility and Awareness

First of all, Paul mentioned humility. He asked them to walk worthy of their calling with all humility. Humility is one of those classic virtues of the Christian faith. As we go through the Bible, both Old and New Testaments, we discover God's emphasis on humility. If we had to define it, we would say humility involves several different aspects. First, it's a self-awareness of our own inadequacy. Oh, someone may brag on us, and don't we love it. But we know ourselves; I know me, and I have neither wings nor a halo. What people think is not necessarily who we are or what we're like. In any given community of believers, people would rather not share who they've been and what they've done.

Humility is the realization I have of who I am and what I am. I like what a man said in a church I once pastored. He heard someone announce that the bishop of the Methodist Church would be present at a meeting. This ole man leaned back in his chair and said, "Well, the bishop doesn't impress me that much. He gets into his pants the same way I get in mine, unless he hangs them up and jumps in them." Kentuckians have a unique way of saying things.

What he said was: "Hey, wait a minute, folks, the bishop has a title, but he's a man. Like all men, he has his faults and failings." Humility is a self-awareness of our own inadequacies. When we are critical of other people, we ought to stop long enough to remember what we ourselves are lacking in certain areas of our lives.

So when Paul urged them to be humble, he had a second point. He also wanted them to be aware of the worth of other people. Humility is not only knowing my own inadequacies, but it's also to know your worth to God. I'm not the only man on God's list. I trust that I've never stood behind the pulpit in all the years I've pastored and felt I am better than anybody in the room. Humility is the recognition that your value to God means as much as my value to God. The worth of every individual life is important. So humility means we're aware of our inadequacies and we aware of other people's worth.

Gentleness and Patience

The second word Paul used was gentleness. In any culture around Israel they considered neither humility nor gentleness a virtue. In the Greco-Roman world the idea of being meek or gentle was to admit you were inferior in character. People counted as virtuous those who presented themselves as self-assured, the confident ones who stayed on top. Again and again, this word gentleness kept popping up, along with meekness and mildness. It can be translated several different ways. I think of three meanings in that one word we need to observe.

First is the word courtesy. Gentleness is a matter of being courteous to other people. That's where mildness comes in. We are courteous to other people in spite of the fact we may not agree with them or even like them. Courtesy demands respect. For example, it seems to me, whether you like someone or not, believe in their principles or not, there comes a point where you simply recognize the courtesy due other people.

For example, in the deaths of Tony Snow, White House Press Secretary, and Jesse Helms, U.S. Senator, the media reports contained many discourteous remarks, slandering the character of these two public figures.[14] Those reports were unnecessary. Courtesy is one of those important virtues, a sense of consideration for people.

I'm not saying we agree with everyone, and neither did Paul. We exhibit gentleness especially in the body of Christ, for to trump our individual interest goes against a concern for the common good. People in church could take note: in order to be a shepherd of sheep, you have to learn to like the smell of sheep. Sometimes we stink, and I'm not talking about needing a shower. We can act in some stinky ways and have some stinky ideas. If you don't believe that, you should read some letters I've received. You know what that tells me? We're just all common folks.

Paul also wrote about patience, and patience is a rich word. What does patience mean to you? Two things it ought to mean. First, steadfastness in times of difficulty. I get weary of hearing people say, "This terrible event happened. Where's God? He allowed all of this." Perhaps you've said something similar. *Where Is God When It Hurts?*[15] is the title of one book. The last time I thought about it: God is exactly where He's always been.

The real question behind this is: "Why should I suffer?" But sometimes I know why I should. Because suffering is what makes me into the person God wants me to be. If I had a lifetime of nothing but ease and pleasure, I can guarantee you my character would be much different than it is today. It's when I've gone through those tough times, when I felt like the bottom had fallen out, and I didn't see how I could manage another day—maybe it was financial or job situations, family or physical problems—every one of those gave me opportunity to be molded and shaped into what God wants me to be.

Stop and think about it: How do you form and forge a piece of iron or steel? You get it red hot and then it's malleable. You've seen the blacksmith in old western movies as he hammered out the horse shoes. He got it hot enough to be flexible enough to beat into shape. That's what God does with us. Sometimes we're so hardheaded we don't hear Him until the bottom falls out. Then when we're down on our knees, God says, "I've been waiting for you. I've got some lessons to teach you."

Through those difficult times God molds and shapes us. I've repeatedly said that the greatest growth period in my life spiritually was the worst period of time I ever went through, and I wouldn't want to go through it again for all the money you can collect. I ended up in a three-month sabbatical trying to get my head screwed on straight again, but during that time and what followed, God did a wonderful work in my life. I am the man I am today, and I thank God for that privilege of suffering. You misunderstood me if you thought I said, "I'm glad for it." There was no joy; there was no picnic. But God used it.

So patience is steadfastness in the tough times. Anybody can get along when everything is going right. When you're rolling on the top of the heap, you don't need anything or anyone. You can take care of life by yourself. But when you hit the bottom, you're malleable for God to mold and shape—if in patience you are allowing Him to do what needs to be done for you.

Wrongdoing and Revenge

On the other side of the coin (there is another side) patience also means we're slow in avenging those wrongdoings we've experienced. You may know people who have done wrong; and you may presently know someone who's hurt you, and you've said to yourself: "I'll never have anything to do with that person again." Mistake! You're in the body of Christ, aren't you? I like what a friend said, "Every person deserves a second chance, or even a third chance."

It's strange to me that in church, the body of Christ, filled with people who rejoice because God has taken them out of all of their foulness, stinkiness, and lostness, and brought them into the kingdom of God, we are sometimes so intolerant and unforgiving of other people who have also fallen. Why? We did our share on the other side of the coin. Not one of us can say there's nothing wrong in anything I've ever done.

The church ought to be a place where broken people come and are welcome. Even when you know they've come out of a broken situation, you love them. Why? Because you have been loved. When I came to World Gospel Church in 1989, I was wounded. People tolerated me, they loved me, they trusted me; and those years proved to be a wonderful experience for me. So, why don't we do that for everyone? Paul promoted patience. We can do the same with ourselves and with others.

Tolerance and Differences

The last word Paul used in this opening passage was tolerance: "bearing with one another in love" (Ephesians 4:2). Simply put, that means putting up with other people's idiosyncrasies. You've heard someone describe a person by saying, "Boy, he's a strange duck." When's the last time you looked in a mirror? To others you may be a strange duck too. All of us have some strange character traits. Each of us is different in a lot of ways. My wife happens to be far more outgoing than I am. I'm more of an inside person. I'm much like my father, a railroad worker, a quiet man. Ann and I planned a three-week vacation by train and it was great. She was as happy as could be, and I went along with her. I enjoyed it, but I was ready to be back home. We're different.

You're different from the people around you. It might be your husband or wife, and you'd say, "Yeah, we're not cut out of the same piece of cloth." Paul talked about tolerance, putting up with one another. Why? Because of love, he said. That's the strongest motive of all. I've come to love my wife, and it hasn't taken our whole married life for me to get there. Love is the strongest influence when it comes to tolerating other people.

What if we'd work at being a church that loves one another? Why not? The church filled with people who love each other will find people beating down the doors to get in. Why? Because the world isn't like that. The world does not show love. Because we are the body of Christ, we are loved and we love others.

Keep the Unity

Along with the personal virtues comes the collective effort which we put into the body of Christ.

Paul wrote that we strive to "keep the unity of the Spirit through the bond of peace" (Ephesians 4:3). We (you and I) have to work at it. We have to work at it collectively, with one another. We *strive* to do this. This word is a strong one; we "make every effort" (v.3). It means there's a relentless resolution to make this work. The secret to a happy marriage is when you're bound and determined to make it work. For if you're looking for a way out, you'll find one. Whether it's a marriage or the church, it will work, but I didn't say it would be easy.

Paul urged those people to strive and keep at it, to hang on. Make sure the unity of the Spirit of God is within the body of Christ. Sometimes we want to throw up both our hands and quit. But in our serious, spiritual moments, we know that's not the way. We make the church *be* the church, because what binds our hearts together is "the unity of the Spirit through the bond of peace" (v. 3). It's the glue that holds us together.

Two other lessons I'd like you to jot down. First are the factors that make unity possible. The second is about the singularity that mandates unity. In verses four through six: "There is one body and one Spirit, just as you were called to one hope when you were called; one Lord, one faith, one baptism; one God and father of all, who is over all, and through all and in all." One,

one, one—repeated seven times. If there is one, then there can't be two, and here's where we get divided among our denominations.

We are divided over our theology, and believe me, I am as intense about my theology as anyone else. But the bottom line for the body of Christ is that we cannot slay each other over our differences. Rather, we seek to love each other and seek peace in spite of our differences. That's a tough job. That's why I believe it's a collective effort but with a singularity, meaning the church has to be one. One Lord, one faith, one baptism, one God and Father. If there's only one way, then why are we cutting these pieces into what's called Methodists, Baptists, Presbyterians, Episcopalians, and Roman Catholics? We can't even name all of the groups. Please don't misunderstand, I haven't said we agree on everything; and I don't say we shouldn't feel intensely about what we believe. Neither should we find ourselves isolated until we're the only ones we think are right.

I believe I'm right in my theology. If I didn't think it was right, I'd change it. If you didn't believe you're right, you'd change also. Because you and I may see things differently does not mean we destroy the unity that's ours in Christ.

In the next section, Paul wrote about diversity that contributes to unity. God has given different gifts to people who work in the church: some apostles, some prophets, some evangelists, some pastors and teachers. I like the way he put those last two together because that's my job; I've been a pastor and a teacher. We see the diversity; we're not all the same, and thank God. I'm glad I don't look like my friend Mike; and he is glad he doesn't look like me. We're different, not only in the way we look. What binds us together is the love of Christ, and that's the way the church functions. So diversity is here to stay, and we're thankful.

Dangers to Unity

Look in verse fourteen in this fourth chapter and you'll find three dangers that prove unity essential:

Then we will no longer be infants, tossed back and forth by the waves, and blown here and there by every wind of teaching and by the cunning and craftiness of people in their deceitful scheming.

One danger is immaturity, because it renders believers unstable and vulnerable. We don't want to stay too close to the door where we got in or we'll find ourselves like children, blown to and from by every wind of doctrine.

The second danger is the deceitfulness we sometimes face. A lie repeated often enough undermines the truth. Because something is taught in universities doesn't make it true. I've said it before: "Don't believe anything I say because I said it. Go to the word of God. If it doesn't verify what I say, don't believe me."

The last point concerns false teachers, for they can wreak havoc upon new believers. All through the ages, people have been moved by false teachers. I saw this in the Methodist Church in which I grew up. The people who took a liberal view of the Bible became seminary professors who trained pastors. They weren't dumb, because now we find a number of those pastors in churches and they don't hold the Scriptures to be the word of God and Jesus Christ as the Son of God. Paul wrote to be aware of false teachers.

What we need is to walk worthy of our calling, strive for unity and peace, and beware of the dangers confronting us. All this we do together in love. Remember also that "to each one of us grace has been given" (Ephesians 4:7).

Prayer: Lord, we pray for ourselves. Forgive us when we sometimes strike out at others because they don't agree with us. Help us not to de-Christianize one another. Lord, we need to be reminded we're not the only Christians in town. In other churches are people You love, and they love You and seek to walk in Your ways.

We pray, Father, that we'll never forget the body of Christ is much larger than our own chosen community. Help us to be one—loving one another, striving for peace, and seeking to manifest those virtues Paul wrote about—to walk pleasingly before Christ who has loved us and called us to Himself. We confess, Father, we've been critical. If we're going to be the faithful people You want us to be, we need to be reminded we're not all cut out of the same cloth. Our differences exist and they determine our decisions. But we all have the same Lord and the same faith. In You we place our allegiance. Amen.

CHAPTER FIVE

The Church as the Body of Christ

Part C: One Body in Christ
Romans 12:4–5

"The Church is a community of believers committed to the dynamic rule of God under the Lordship of Jesus Christ. The exercise of the powers of the kingdom bears witness to the fact of redemption and the work of the Holy Spirit in redemptive enterprise to which the Church has been called" (W.B.C.).

Patch Adams, in his book *House Calls*,[16] wrote about the importance of community. Paul also wrote about community in the twelfth chapter of his letter to the Romans:

For just as each of us has one body with many members, and these members do not all have the

same function, so in Christ we, though many, form one body, and each member belongs to all the others.
—Romans 12:4–5

As you may well believe, the early Christians viewed community as extremely important, particularly as they began to move out into a society that did not understand the church's message and often responded in hostility to the gospel. Those Christians found their consolation and encouragement in one another, and they leaned heavily upon the body of believers. They depended upon community. The same is true for us today, in spite of the fact the church's PR doesn't rate high. Years ago a poll conducted in *US News and World Report* rated people's confidence in various matters like government. The level of confidence people had in organized religion was then at twenty-seven percent. That isn't good, no matter how old the report is.

What Patch Adams said about the value of community and the health process[16] connects with how important community was in the New Testament. We cannot pass over Paul's words and ignore them. Many of those who rank in the percentage of having no confidence in the church are not anti-Christ; they're anti-church. The church has projected a poor image in the eyes of the world. Some reasons are obvious.

Denominations and Divisions

First, the church is divided within itself and much of the fighting that goes on in terms of the Christian faith happens between varying denominations and groups. We are constantly leveling down on one another, and as a consequence we have not presented to the world a community of believers, but a fragmented bunch of people.

Lesslie Newbigin wrote *The Finality of Christ*.[17] Newbigin spent many years as a missionary in India and became the bishop of Madras in the Anglican Church. His appeal to American missionaries went something like this: "Please don't bring to India all of the divisions that divide you in America. We don't need them" (my words).

During my work on teams for the Emmaus Walk, I've been impressed that when the focus is upon Christ, superficial church issues fade into insignificance. I had a young man grab my arm one weekend and ask, "Can I talk to you?" We pulled away from the group. He used to attend church when he was a kid, but his family got away from the church and he had not been involved in church for a long time. He joined the Roman Catholic Church and made a commitment of his life to Christ. The whole point of his pulling me aside was to say he would go back to his church and say they don't need to be afraid of the Emmaus Walk, for it's a place where Christians can be one. That's the reason why I've been actively involved in the Emmaus community and why I urge people to consider taking part in this experience. People come out of various backgrounds and put aside their differences, because Jesus Christ is Lord and everything else takes second place.

However much we may divide ourselves, when I listen to the apostle Paul, the many are one body. Even though we're not monolithic in our ideas, seeing all issues the same way, the body of Christ is not divided. Why then does the world feel as it does toward the church? First of all, it's because of our divisions and squabbles among those who profess to be followers of Christ. Second, we have insisted the world recognize high ethical standards, but we, as church members, have often failed to live up to them. People should be able to notice the teachings of Jesus Christ are what our world needs. Look what it's doing for His people.

Jesus understood the importance of modeling, setting an example. They gathered in the upper room and He took off His outer garment, wrapped a towel around His waist, and washed the feet of the disciples. Afterward He said, "Do you understand what I have done for you? . . . I have set you an example that you should do as I have done for you" (John 13:12, 15). Too often we have high-sounding theological terms and ideas, but these great morals and principles fail to be converted into everyday routines of our lives. If we don't live it, how can we expect the world to appreciate or respect the church?

Institutions and Individuals

Third, institutionalization has often given the church a poor image. I saw an article with the title "Poop and Circumstance." Having been on a college campus where we heard *Pomp and Circumstance* played as we marched in every graduation, that title caught my attention. Perhaps people view us in the church as a lot of poop and circumstance with not much relevance to address their lives and meet needs. If we do not convert the message of Jesus Christ into actions to reach where people live and hurt, then church will not make much difference to them. People are not looking for form and ritual which freezes us into a mold; they are looking at us to represent lives transformed by a Savior. Paul said, though we are many, we are one. We are the body of Christ, and a body is alive.

Another issue: we have a radical individualization in our day. We've become fragmented: We hold the idea in America that one's private opinions are as good as anyone else's opinions. We've lost a sense of authority. John Stott wrote a book for preachers entitled *Between Two Worlds*.[18] We're standing in that world today, a world often marred by the lack of authority. Even in the church, we have the idea that none of us have the right to insist truth has authority over what we are and say and think and do. We've received a bad image from the charlatans who are more power brokers than prophets. The world sees a distorted image of the church. Public news reported about a pastor, the head of his denomination, who had misused four million dollars. We have as many scoundrels inside as they have outside, so why should we rate any consideration?

When the apostle Paul turned to the church, he saw it as tremendously significant to Christians. Paul also said we are diversified; we do not all have the same gifts. With all our differences we come together in unity; for the body has parts yet it is one. We are one body, not a number of bodies. When we look at the image Paul created for us—the church as one body—what did it mean to Paul and what does it mean to us today?

We are the body of Christ in the sense Christ is the reason for our existence. There's no other reason. There's no reason for you and me to meet on a Sunday morning except for Jesus Christ. What makes us the body of Christ is Christ Himself:

the single distinction between our lives and the unbelieving world. It's important what Jesus has done for us. We understand it's not who I am or how much I have or what I do. It's not our gifts, it's not what we can do, and it's not how much money collectively we can raise for some cause. The only factor that makes the church the body of Christ is what Jesus Christ has done in us individually and personally. That truth binds us together.

We're different from one another; we don't look or think alike. So what unites us in worship? We sing a song about binding us together with chords of love.[19] We are redeemed not because we're good; we are redeemed in spite of the fact we were sinful. We are made into new creations in Christ, and we are gathered here in one accord. Jesus Christ has transformed us; we have received forgiveness through the shed blood of Christ and reconciliation with God. Paul wrote: "in Christ we, though many, form one body, and each member belongs to all the others" (Romans 12:5).

The Church and Its Ministry

We are a community. We are a body because Jesus is the head and as members, parts of the body, we surrender to His head. We worship together in order to listen to Christ. It is not the pastor who calls the shots or has the right to determine the course for the future direction of the church. Christ is the head of the Church, the big C Church. Christ is the reason for our existence.

We belong to Christ. The church does not belong to its members. Pastors sometimes say, "Let me tell you about *my* church." Yet the church belongs to Christ. Lay people sometimes talk about *my* church. It may be the one you attend, but it doesn't belong to you either. It belongs to Christ. The church also doesn't belong to a denomination. The church is Christ's body. In Him every believer is made one, whatever may be the denominational tag hung on a particular person or church.

One of the refreshing joys I've found in the Emmaus community is when I can get together with people who have no denominational affili-ation with me. And often they are people with whom I disagree in terms of theological distinc-tions. But we lay those differences aside to unite in "one Lord, one faith, one baptism; one God and Father of all, who is over all and through all and in all" (Ephesians 4:5-6). We are controlled by Christ and we are His body.

It goes farther. As the body of Christ, we are the extension of Christ. At Christmas we celebrate God who became incarnate in Jesus Christ. But we can't forget when Jesus ascended to heaven, His message to the church was that *we* are now the incarnation of God's message to an unbelieving world. Luke started His introduction to the book of Acts by reminding the church to continue what Jesus began to teach and to do. As the incarnation of Christ, our ministry is to continue His ministry.

What was Christ's ministry? To suffer for the redemption of the world. Who in the world joins an organization to suffer? You join an organization for fun or for civic service. To join a group in order to suffer is absolutely unheard of; it's preposterous and yet it's the mission of the church. Paul said, "I fill up in my flesh what is still lacking in regard to Christ's afflictions, for the sake of his body, which is the church" (Colossians 1:24). We ask God, "How do we reach our world for You?" God has called us to suffer. It doesn't mean we'll necessarily die on a cross or burn at a stake, although many have done so. It does mean we are not to look for convenience and comfort.

We watch a football game and see a man who may be agonizing in his body, yet he puts himself out on the field for the sake of a team, to win the game. Too often in church if we move outside our comfort zone, we think: *Well, I didn't bargain for that!* A man is willing to suffer for a football game, but we don't want to be inconvenienced for a lost world.

Missionaries enjoy serving Jesus, and they wouldn't do otherwise. But don't kid yourself, missionaries suffer. While on the mission field Christmas and Easter, birthdays and anniversaries roll around, and their families are separated. They are isolated from everyone who's near and dear to them. Why are they there? There's only one reason. The church's ministry is to reach a lost world, and sometimes it means suffering—not always comfortable and convenient.

The Bible teaches about giving sacrificially, but are we willing to accept that? People say the New Testament doesn't teach about tithing. If we became tithers to His kingdom, local churches would not have to call meetings to discover how they can raise funds for working in Jesus' name. Jesus said we ought to give of ourselves, and if it creates a bit of inconvenience, it's part of being members of the body of Christ. And that's all right. Yes, it may inconvenience us; it may hurt a bit. Christ suffered on a cross for the redemption of the world, and I am to continue His ministry.

Our ministry is the redemption of the world, and the world begins at our doorstep. It's not enough for a church to send money to people overseas when we have people in our own community who need the gospel of Jesus Christ. That's the responsibility of the church. We should send missionaries around the world, yes, but we cannot ignore those who are in our community. Christ's body, the church, is responsible for the ministry of carrying His name, to continue His teaching, to reach the ends of the earth, beginning at our doorstep.

Transformed, Not Conformed

The church is, after all, a human community. Sure, the church has problems, because the church is made up of people. Problems don't hang out there in the air; people come with problems. When you and I joined the church, we brought problems with us, and often the biggest problem is ourselves. The church is made up of people who are being transformed by Jesus Christ, and we profess to be His disciples. Have we completed all God desires of us? Can we say we're the perfect community? I can only tell you I'm being transformed daily. You didn't know me sixty years ago and you don't know what goes on in my day-to-day life. The power of the gospel transforms you and me. We are believers whose minds and hearts are being renewed.

The world may call the church a bunch of hypocrites; but if you're a citizen of the United States, it would be difficult to say there are no hypocrites in the government. So where do you go? The Lions Club? The Civitans? The Elks? In those groups, is everyone crystal clear and with no role players? No. Paul wrote to the Corinthians that they should not fellowship with unbelievers and people guilty of immorality. He wasn't talking about the world, because if they were not to associate with them, they would have to leave the world. (See 2 Corinthians 6:14-18.) Are there hypocrites in church? Yes. Are we glad they're here? Absolutely, because they'll never be other than a hypocrite unless they meet Jesus. They're not going to meet Jesus in an unbelieving world; they can meet Him in church.

I heard E. Stanley Jones emphasize this passage in Second Corinthians in a different way. In essence, he said we are "becoming Christians." I thought: *No, we're not becoming Christian; we are either Christians or we're not Christians.* Then I found that's exactly what the Greek said, written in present tense. We are becoming Christ-like. Jesus told the Pharisees, "It is not the healthy who need a doctor, but the sick. I have not come to call the righteous, but sinners to repentance" (Luke 5:31-32). Yes, we are people who are becoming—we are *being* transformed, not conformed to this present age. Through setting priorities and purposes we accomplish the goal to be Christ-like.

Friends, don't ever apologize for not being perfect. If you ever told somebody we were perfect, then you'd have to repent of lying. At least we know where we're trying to go and we're leaning on Christ who is able to make us like Himself.

We're a human community with faults and failures. We walk God's straight and narrow way, and sometimes in our weaknesses we surrender to some despicable, unworthy traits.

I love one stanza in Harry E. Fosdick's hymn *God of Grace and God of Glory*.[20] I once wrote it across the top of my calendar: "Save us from weak resignation to the evils we deplore." That's our cry. We are imperfect. Do we make mistakes and have we committed sins? Unfortunately and to our shame we admit it's true, but we're still the body of Christ. We are not a perfect body but a body of humans in the process of becoming. We reflect in our being the various levels of our sanctification and our sinfulness.

Someone who accepts Jesus as Savior today is not instantaneously born as a saint in any perfect sense of the term. We are in process, folks. God is making a difference in my life, for I'm not the man I used to be. I praise God I'm also not the man one day I hope to be, for I anticipate God's continuous work in my life. Yes, we are a human bunch, but God has called us to do His work. We're not perfect, but we're the body of Christ brought together as His church.

Outreach of Community

The other side of the coin is we see only imperfectly now. We're praying for a kingdom to come and a will to be done. We're not praying for a moral kingdom but a holy kingdom. It's going to be the beauty of it, not the correctness of it, as Evelyn Underhill wrote.[21] God's eternal kingdom will bring the fulfillment of all those aspirations having been born in us by our relationship to Jesus Christ. There is coming a day when our imperfections will fall aside and we'll find that God is perfect and not only adequate. We'll also find His kingdom is ruled by charity, not by law. That kingdom's coming, but we are now a part of the body of Christ, a human community reaching out for what God wants us to be. When we accept Jesus as our Lord, we want to be a part of His church.

God made the early church a witness, an instrument in His hands to evangelize the world. Our witness is still the mission of the church. All we have to share with others is the overflow of our own personal lives. In John's Gospel, when Jesus was talking about people receiving the Holy Spirit, He said, "rivers of living water will flow from within them" (7:38). God wants to take ordinary people, give them a living experience of Himself so they can speak only what they've seen and heard. We have Christ's message to tell a lost world.

We bring our tithes and offerings to church. Some joke and say: "The church is always after money." How much does it cost anyone to attend church on any given day? Go to an NBA or NFL game this afternoon and see whether they let you come in at no cost. Rack up the totals of what you spend on hobbies, entertainment, and fun stuff. Evidently they don't give that stuff away. You can come into any church without paying.

We give our tithes and offerings not because anyone brow beats us or twists our arms, but because we belong to Christ. We want to see the kingdom come, and we want the church to reach out and do its job. We give to missions, because we believe people in other countries who don't know about Christ need someone there to tell them. Churches expand their facilities in order to reach out and pull people in. For example, a well-equipped nursery wing could be a place where parents can say, "This is a wonderful place. I can bring our kids here." We want to light up the lives of children, because their lights will shine for a generation. Yes, we want to worship God in a beautiful sanctuary because He is beautiful, and we want to offer Him the very best.

We do all this, because we're the body of Christ. We sing for Him. We praise Him. We pray to Him. What then does it mean for us today? As the body of Christ, we worship Him. We sing, "He is Lord, He is Lord, He is risen from the dead, and He is

Lord."[22] We bow our knees to worship Him as King of kings and Lord of lords. Because we are the body of Christ, we seek to serve Him—to know God's will and to walk in it. We pray to have the vision God wants us to have so we can see what tasks are immediately before us and by God's grace we are able to accomplish. We are the people of God and He is Lord and we belong to Him. In a lost world with no direction, we thank God through Jesus Christ there is a goal toward which we are moving and the fulfillment of all aspirations God put in us when He placed eternity in our hearts. We are the body of Christ. We, though many, are one. May it be so.

Prayer: Lord Jesus, the only reason we are in church is because of You and the impact You've had upon us as individuals. We're not in church as simply a good token of appreciation. We're not here because it's a beautiful place. We are here to allow You, Lord, to be the head of the body, the church, those who love and serve You as members of that body. We seek to accomplish Your purposes and continue Your teachings, given us by Your example as well as by Your words. In spite of our different gifts, abilities, and understanding, and in spite of the fact we're not all alike: we are one. As the parts of our physical body are different in function and appearance, it's also true of us as a church. We want to be Your body in our local churches and in the Church universal.

We thank You, Father, for You loved us so much You gave Your Son to die on a cross so that He could produce a body of redeemed people to be in right relationship with You, to be Your people.

As we remember Your suffering, Lord Jesus, make us willing to be whatever You call us to be, to serve You in our present age. We pray in Your holy name. Amen.

CHAPTER SIX

Secrets of a Dynamic Church

Observations on the First-century Church
Part A: A Praying Church
Acts 4:23–35

"The Church is the 'called-out' people of God, who have been bought with a price, even the blood of Jesus Christ. Recognizing the value and worth of collective effort, they are banded together as a redemptive society with missionary visions of evangelizing the world for Jesus Christ" (W.B.C.).

Introduction

When I was a young preacher, I thought the greatest experience would have been to be part of the early church, for surely it must have been a perfect institution. Then I started reading the Bible and found out it wasn't true.

So what made the first-century church such a dynamic influence in the world? God took a group of people, common ordinary people, and made them into the instrument of His word. And since the early church was made up of people like us, that makes it even more phenomenal.

William Arthur wrote *The Tongue of Fire*, first published in 1858.[23] Basically it was a book for ministers, emphasizing the need to proclaim God's word with the same effectiveness as did the early church. Arthur said God could have done one of two things in establishing the church. He could have used extraordinary people or he could have taken ordinary people and filled them with extraordinary power. God did the latter. He took ordinary people, filled them with extraordinary power, and made them useful in the work of His kingdom.

As I've stated, I'm satisfied that one of the greatest miracles in the Bible and in history is the miracle of the existence of the church. Stop to think: one hundred twenty disorganized and sometimes disgruntled people met in the upper room on the day of Pentecost when the Holy Spirit came upon them. From those insignificant beginnings the existence of a movement started that would shake the world. In fact, it has shaken all of human history for over 2000 years and even to the present day. And in spite of all that would militate against its existence, the church is still here.

The book of Acts has given us a wide angle shot of what God did in the first century through those ordinary people. It reached out and captured in a still photograph all of the enthusiasm and tremendous power being manifested in the lives of those people. How could anyone read the book of Acts and question the first century church was a dynamic church?

Wouldn't it have been wonderful to be there in Jerusalem, at the temple, when Peter looked at that man, lame, lying at the gate, and said to him, "Silver or gold I do not have, but what I do have I give you. In the name of Jesus Christ of Nazareth, walk" (Acts 3:6)? Wouldn't it have been exciting to be part of that gallant band of early disciples who went all over the known world to share the good news that God so loved the world?

The early church was a dynamic church, but not because it was composed of perfect Christians. Nor was it because those early disciples had any lack of problems. One has only to read the book of First Corinthians to see their troubles were many and their struggles were more than we would like to have.

Let's look at the book of Acts, chapter four. We break into the story when the Sanhedrin released Peter and John after their arrest by the Sadducees for "proclaiming in Jesus the resurrection of the dead" (Acts 4:2). This happened on the heels of healing the man at the Gate Beautiful. The Sanhedrin threatened them never again to preach in the name of Jesus. But Peter and John responded: "Which is right in God's eyes: to listen to you, or to him? You be the judges! As for us, we cannot help speaking about what we have seen and heard" (4:19–20).We pick up the story at that point in Acts 4:23.

On their release, Peter and John went back to their own people and reported all that the chief priests and the elders had said to them. When they heard this, they raised their voices together in prayer to God. "Sovereign Lord," they said, "you made the heavens and the earth and the sea, and everything in them. You spoke by the Holy Spirit through the mouth of your servant, our father David: 'Why do the nations rage and the peoples plot in vain? The kings of the earth rise up and the rulers band together against the Lord and against his anointed one.' Indeed Herod and Pontius Pilate met together with the Gentiles and the people of Israel in this city to conspire against your holy servant Jesus, whom you anointed. They did what your power and will had decided beforehand

should happen. Now, Lord, consider their threats and enable your servants to speak your word with great boldness. Stretch out your hand to heal and perform signs and wonders through the name of your holy servant Jesus." After they prayed, the place where they were meeting was shaken. And they were all filled with the Holy Spirit and spoke the word of God boldly. All the believers were one in heart and mind. No one claimed that any of their possessions was their own, but they shared everything they had. With great power the apostles continued to testify to the resurrection of the Lord Jesus. And God's grace was so powerfully at work in them all that there were no needy persons among them. For from time to time those who owned land or houses sold them, brought the money from the sales and put it at the apostles' feet, and it was distributed to anyone who had need.
—Acts 4:23–35

In this tremendous passage, and in other places in the book of Acts, we find one aspect of the secret of the early church. Let's glean the reasons God used them. If these characteristics made them dynamic in the first century, would not these same concepts make us effective today? How can the church be the instrument God wants it to be? Step it back and ask, "How can I be the kind of person I ought to be?" for the church is never anything other than what we as individuals are. When I discover what made the early church God's instrument, this ought to be the goal and object for my life spiritually, so I can be the person God wants me to be.

Confidence in Prayer

Out of this chapter from the book of Acts, I suggest three objectives which I trust are helpful as we think about our own Christian lives. I begin with the most obvious: namely they were a praying people. Let's look on the surface and then to what leads us a bit deeper.

First, some surface observations. When they released Peter and John, these two men first went back to their group and held a prayer meeting. For us prayer is often the last resort rather than our first priority. They didn't say, "When everything else fails, then we'll pray." They got out of prison and they prayed first. In our own personal lives, do we pray when we ought to pray?

In a biography of Andrew Murray, he reported about being with preachers in South Africa. He first asked how many of them prayed thirty minutes or longer a day. Out of those two hundred preachers, he got a smattering show of hands. Then he asked how many of them prayed fifteen minutes or longer each day. A few more raised their hands. When he got down to asking how many prayed five minutes a day, he received a generous show of hands. Those persons were in the ministry. When we ask ourselves how much time we spend praying, we're automatically introduced to what is one of the greatest problem areas in our spiritual lives. We do not pray.

For example, when we start cutting out services in the church, what's the first casualty? Prayer meeting. If there's one service that should be maintained, it's prayer meeting. We could better afford to do away with Sunday morning service than dismiss prayer meeting. You may want to argue with me, but I believe the secret of power in our lives personally, and the secret of the church, is to be found in the fact that we pray.

We can never recite all we need to say about prayer, even if we knew everything needed to be said. In my own spiritual life, the area where I feel the weakest is the matter of prayer. There's much I don't understand about prayer. There's much I've only now begun to comprehend.

My uncle, a Methodist preacher, said to me when I began my ministry, "If I could go and start over again, the one thing I would change is to pray more." Now as I look at my life, I have to confess, "How tragic. I'm now ready to state what my uncle

said, and yet it was a long time ago when he confessed to me." I simply do not pray like I ought.

Those disciples immediately called a prayer
meeting and began to pray. What was it that
made their kind of vital praying possible? I'm led
to draw several conclusions, surface conclusions
I call them. First of all, they must have had a tremendous confidence in prayer. If we believe in the
power of prayer, we would utilize it more. Perhaps
we do not have confidence in prayer like we ought.
We've seen the motto on a plaque: "Prayer Changes
Things." Do we believe it? If we believed it, then
why don't we exercise power to change things?

We're always talking about how desperately
needy the world is, about how the devil has the
whole thing in a sack in a downhill pull. You'd
think the church's mission is to sit around and pray,
"Come, Lord Jesus, and come quickly." Instead, we
ought to assault the world in Jesus' name. Perhaps
we lack the necessary power to do so. I've been
reproved in my own life, and I've changed my pattern of prayer. I'm more intent on this business. I
don't want regrets about my prayer life. The disciples prayed, and yet the early church was imperfect. It was made up of ordinary individuals, like
you and me. But they did pray.

While reading through the New Testament, I've
underlined the occurrences of prayer. I wanted

to assimilate this in my thinking and understand more of the dynamic and significance of prayer for spiritual life. They had confidence in prayer. They prayed because they believed prayer made a difference.

Confidence in God

Secondly, the disciples had confidence in prayer because they had confidence in the One to whom they were praying. Theirs was a confidence in God. They prayed to "Sovereign Lord" (Acts 4:24), how the Greek is translated. One word for Lord in the Greek is *Kurios*, the word occurring most of the time. But there is another Greek word translated Lord and it's used here. It's the word *despotes*, from which we get the English word "despot," a person who has absolute authority and power. The disciples were in a jam. They were face to face with the Sanhedrin who threatened them never again to speak in the name of Jesus. It was no idle threat. The religious leaders had killed Jesus. Soon they would kill Stephen.

Peter and John went back and called a prayer meeting. They looked to God, and how did they address Him? They addressed Him as *despotes*, Sovereign Lord. They addressed God with the full realization He had ultimate control and authority over everything that exists. If you believe God is sovereign, it's easy to call upon Him. It's easy to pray, because God does make a difference in our lives. They had confidence in prayer, because they had confidence in the One to whom they prayed.

Confidence in Relationship

I want to take it up a third step: they had confidence in the One to whom they prayed, because they had confidence in their relationship with Him. Paul Little in his book, *Know Why You Believe*,[24] wrote: "Hitler's slaughter of six million Jews was based on a sincere view of race supremacy, but he was desperately wrong." If God were like Adolph Hitler, we know how we would respond. Worship would be like many pagan religions: seeking to appease the gods, seeking to escape the terror of their wrath, seeking to avert tremendous potential danger in their existence. But when the disciples prayed, they prayed in confidence because Jesus had taught them when they came to God, they addressed him as Father.

H. W. F. Gesenius, German scholar, has suggested the most unique teaching Jesus gave His disciples was to approach God with the term "Abba," the Aramaic word akin to the English word for "Daddy." Jesus taught them to come not with the more formal Hebrew word *avi'ad,* my Father. This has a corollary in my own life. I never addressed my father as Father. He was always Daddy to me. Daddy is more intimate and personal than Father. Gesenius was saying: This is what Jesus revealed to the disciples. He caused them to see their relationship with God was one of a child to their Daddy. Since that is true, no wonder they felt confident to come and pray.

It almost sounds blasphemous, doesn't it, if we were to pray like that? "Daddy, who art in heaven." That sounds fake, and yet that's because we've lost the sense of intimacy. Those disciples believed in prayer because they believed in God, and they could believe in God because of the relationship established between them and God through Jesus Christ.

That's why in *My Utmost for His Highest,* Oswald Chambers[25] said God answers prayer on the ground of redemption. Every answer to prayer God brings is an answer made possible because of Christ's redeeming love in our lives. That's what it means in the New Testament to pray in Jesus' name. I've heard people recite that almost as if it were a magical formula: "in Jesus' name." We've said the formula, now it's going to happen. It's not about saying a formula, but it's coming through redeeming grace that's ours in Christ. "God, the Father of our Lord Jesus Christ, who has blessed us in the heavenly realms with every spiritual blessing in Christ"

(Ephesians 1:3). Through our prayers, in Christ, "every spiritual blessing" is available to us.

The love of God brings us closer through Christ His Son and makes it possible for us to be sons and daughters of God through Jesus Christ. My friends, that's exciting news for us. In case we've never realized it fully, our entry into the presence of God is our right to come into His presence and expect He will hear our prayers, and not only hear them but answer them because He is our Father.

When I was academic dean at Asbury College, I knew when students came to my office they wanted something. It was not generally to pass the time of day. But there was this one student, a girl. She would come to my office every once in a while, and she would waltz past my secretary's desk, and if my door was open she'd walk right into my office. More than one time she would come right up to my desk with a load of books in her arms and plop them onto my desk. She'd look at me and she's say, "Hi ya, Pop." Relationship makes all the difference in the world. No other student did that, but she did. Why? She had confidence in our relationship.

Now why do we come to God as "Abba"? Isn't it the confidence we have in our relationship? He is Sovereign Lord, but we have confidence in the relationship we have with Him as our Father's children.

Confidence in Each Other

The early church had confidence in their relationship with God, but I want to press this a bit further. Something else about their praying strikes me. They had confidence in each other.

It doesn't say when Peter and John got out of jail they went back to the group and then everyone went home to their own private closets and began to pray. What it said is they all came together and began to pray. It's that confidence in one another that makes prayer such a dynamic force within the church. I suspect this is perhaps the greatest loss we've experienced. It isn't that none of us pray. Whether from embarrassment or dedication, we would say: "Yes, I prayed this week." While that may be true as individuals, one of the things lost from the church today is corporate prayer, whereas together we become the body of Christ.

A church is not a church until together it becomes His body. And how does it become the body unless the breath of God breathes through it? What happens when we pray together? It's a matter of confidence in prayer, confidence in God, confidence in the relationship one has with God, and corporate confidence in each other.

But I have a second question on my mind. What is it that makes prayer so powerful? Those early disciples saw something in the life of their Lord that made them want to pray, and it was not simply an atmosphere of piety, a religious quality. They saw the power of prayer unleashed in the life of their Lord. When they saw Him pray and saw power being released within His life, they knew prayer was something they could not do without. Through the centuries the church has discovered prayer as a mighty source of power. Let's analyze it.

Prayer Precludes Self-reliance

What makes prayer so powerful? First of all, prayer makes one a powerful disciple, because prayer precludes our self-reliance. Although people belong to the church and even name the name of Christ, one spiritual problem is we think we can somehow make it through these days in and of and by ourselves. As long as we rely upon our own strength, we will not know the power of God working within us.

Have you ever noticed when you begin to pray, something happens? If today we knew of some kind of emergency situation, perhaps the release of a toxic gas threatening to envelop our whole community and people could be physically damaged or lives could be lost. You and I would cancel everything on our schedule. We would get on our knees before God and pray. What captures our minds? I believe it's the sense that we cannot not pray. Something larger than ourselves is at stake.

Until I learn how to offer a prayer that precludes my own sense of self-reliance, I will not know what it is to be a dynamic disciple, and the church will not know what it means to be a dynamic church.

Prayer Perfects Focus

What makes prayer powerful? First, it precludes our self-reliance. Second, it perfects our focus spiritually. You say, what do you mean by that? I mean simply this: One of the great problems we all face is getting everything into focus and getting life laid out in its right perspective. Prayer helps us to accomplish that.

The longer one looks at a problem, the more disproportionate things become until finally we are like those Old Testament spies. Moses sent twelve spies into the land of Israel, and when they returned ten spies said (and I paraphrase): "Oh, the people who live in the Promised Land are giants; it's impossible for us to enter and win any kind of victory. We can't take this land." The longer they stared at the people of Canaan, the bigger they grew and the smaller the Israelites became in their own eyes. (See Numbers 13:17–28.)

You see, their focus was out of proportion. Prayer helps us focus, not upon our problems, but upon God. As I focus upon God, I begin to see myself and my circumstances more clearly. My vision is perfected, and I see things as they ought to be seen.

I don't like wearing glasses. I wish I could go back to what my sight was when I could write those tiny notes and read them all. But it's not possible now. I have to put on glasses to make the focus true. The doctor told me it was presbyopia, which means my eyes are getting old. The eye muscle after a while gets a little tired; so now I need glasses. Prayer is like a pair of glasses. Issues are sort of blurry until I pray. I don't know how or why it works, but it does.

What's interesting in my own life spiritually is I understand more theology than I ever did before. The keenest insights I'm getting in theology are not what comes while I read a book but when I'm on my knees. Prayer perfects our spiritual focus.

Prayer Particularizes Faith

Third, prayer is powerful because it particularizes our faith. That's an important part of our praying. Have you ever noticed how generalized statements are when we recite the Apostles' Creed? "I believe in God, the Father Almighty, Maker of heaven and earth; and in Jesus Christ, His only Son our Lord; who was conceived by the

Holy Spirit, born of the Virgin Mary . . . ."[26] Great theology, but seemingly unrelated to the particulars of my life and your life.

But when I begin to pray and the object of my prayer is a specific need or person or concern, my faith is particularized. It isn't: "Lord, bless the entire world." But it's: "Lord, I need you, and I need you for this reason, and here is my concern. Here is the matter that's blocking my way. Here is the burden that's crushing life out of me. Here is why I'm struggling." Faith bears down on the one place that's important in my life.

We've all watched the little boy as he stands in the school yard with his magnifying glass and piece of paper, and he wiggles them around until he gets the sun directed through the magnifying glass. It's then brought to the right place and particularized to a tiny little speck on the piece of paper, and before long the paper begins to brown; it begins to scorch. Why? The sun has been up there all along, so why does the paper begin to scorch now? You know the answer. Somehow the magnifying glass took all the brilliance of the sun and rather than shine everyplace, it particularized to one spot. Focusing upon one spot, it generated tremendous heat. If we need anything in the church today, we need to particularize our faith until we see specifics in our relationship with God.

W. E. Sangster, in a great sermon, "Covet Earnestly the Best Gift,"[27] explained the value of coveting. He said that the trouble with so many people's lives spiritually is they are "vague in their aim." As long as we're vague in our aim, we never hit anything.

Prayer Promotes Fellowship

Fourth, corporate prayer promotes our fellowship. Have you seen those advertisements for the friendly church? Nothing unique about that. We talk about great fellowship and we try to promote it. But we're missing the one avenue that produces genuine fellowship: the prayer life of the church.

When people pray together, fellowship becomes a reality. Let me go further than that: (and at the risk of being blatantly wrong) I question whether there is any real fellowship in the church until there is fellowship born of prayer. Gimmicks and programs all promote something, but not fellowship. Nothing binds us together in love more than praying together. One of the reasons why the early church loved one another was they prayed together.

When I attended seminary, a fellow student had been a pastor in Philadelphia. He reported that of all the weddings he ever performed, only one divorce happened. Phenomenal then, and it might be near impossible now. As one person has said, the only reason you need for a divorce today is the marriage license. That's bad, and sad. This pastor said, "I urged every couple that before they went to bed each night to get on their knees, join hands, and pray together." He said, "That became the reason for their good marriages. When one person gets down with another person and they pray together, they cannot go to bed angry." I'm not a marriage counselor, but he made good sense. Prayer is also effective in the body of Christ. Prayer promotes fellowship and unity. You can't pray with someone and not love them. Christ's love is evident when we pray together.

Prayer Prevents Faltering

Last, prayer prevents our faltering. What makes prayer so powerful? Without it, I find myself lost in my own insensitivity to God. Unless a regular pattern of praying exists in our lives, we'll find ourselves wandering, not moving specifically in any spiritual direction. Prayer keeps us from stumbling and failing in our relationship with Christ. I say that because it's true in my own life. When I fail to pray, I fail to walk straight spiritually. Prayer is powerful, because without it one tries to go through life alone.

When I get up in the morning to spend the needed time with the Lord, I find the whole day runs not more smoothly, not without problems, not with trouble-free situations, not because everything turns out the way I want, but because it's difficult to forget the relationship I have with Christ. I have begun the day in my relationship with Christ through prayer. That helps to keep me from faltering, from stumbling, and from failing.

Prayer Proves God's Reality

It's one thing to say I believe in God. But I believe in God for what? What does God mean in my life? God does not provide everything I ask Him to do when I pray. I'm glad He doesn't answer all my prayers. If He had answered all my prayers, my spiritual growth would have been limited.

For example, when we moved to One Mission Society in Greenwood, Indiana, we left a house in Wilmore, Kentucky. Like a great weight around our necks, mortgage payments had to be made. For over a year we tried to sell it. I wrestled in prayer, and at times I got absolutely desperate with God for the sale of our house. But God taught me some spiritual lessons I would never have known without that experience.

You know the song "'Tis So Sweet to Trust in Jesus" (Louisa Snead).[28] I sing that song differently today because of the house in Wilmore. You ask, "How does that make sense?" I wrestled through the problem while cutting the grass. You can't do anything else but think when mowing the lawn. I cried out to God in my soul, "Lord, we have to sell our house." It looked like we had a deal, but it fell through. Failure crushed me. In the middle of my thoughts came those words: "Jesus, Jesus, how I trust Him! How I've proved Him o'er and o'er!" Then the last stanza, "I'm so glad I learned to trust Thee, Precious Jesus, Savior, Friend." Where do we learn to trust? It's not when everything runs smoothly. We learn to trust when nothing is going well.

My prayer life has proven the reality of God. Whether things work out the way I want them to or not, God exists. I don't believe in God because He gives me what I want. I believe in God because He is. What happens doesn't change the fact that God is. I've come under the constraint of the object, as John Baillie would say. I believe in God because I cannot not believe in Him. Because He is. My prayers particularize my faith in God in ways I've never known before.

The early church was a dynamic church. Why was it a dynamic church? One of the reasons: they prayed, earnestly and fervently. Without prayer, no church becomes a dynamic church. Prayer is vital as a dynamic in genuine spirituality.

The early church was not a perfect church, but it was a good church. It was made up of good people, ordinary people. God took them and turned the world upside down. If and when the church discovers once again the power of prayer, we will discover the not-so-secret of winning the world for Jesus.

Prayer: Father, I don't know what others desire, but I know I want to ask: Teach me to pray. Lord, teach me how to pray. We acknowledge prayer is not a matter of sophisticated words. We know it isn't a matter of memorizing the right religious formula. And we realize, Lord, that it isn't simply doing our duty. It's more. Lord, teach us how to pray. Teach us to be a praying people. Lord, we want to serve this present age. We want to be a dynamic church so we might truly be the body of Christ in our community. Teach us how to pray. May we begin regularly to form the habit of prayer, because it's only then we learn how to pray and prayer becomes the dynamic it ought to be in our spiritual experience. Help us, each one, Father, to pray as we ought. In Jesus' name. Amen.

CHAPTER SEVEN

Secrets of a Dynamic Church

Observations on the First-century Church
Part B: A Pentecostal Church
Acts 4:29–31

"Any assembly of true Christians is a church. 'For where two or three gather in my name, there am I with them' (Matthew 18:20). The name and the Presence are indispensable to a local church. A group of saved persons, however small, who meet in Christ's name and recognize His Presence, form a true cell in His body and enjoy the full power and authority of Christ Himself" (A. W. Tozer, *The Price of Neglect*).[29]

We're looking again at the passage in Acts, chapter four. Let's notice the conclusion of the prayer those early disciples prayed:

Now, Lord, consider their threats and enable your servants to speak your word with great boldness. Stretch out your hand to heal and perform signs and wonders through the name of your holy servant Jesus. After they prayed, the place where they were meeting was shaken. And they were all filled with the Holy Spirit and spoke the word of God boldly.
—Acts 4:29–31

We found the first of those dynamic secrets of the early church was no secret at all. As we discover again and again in Scripture, prayer plays a vital part in our relationship with God. It's always been true, and it shall always be so. Prayer is a vital concern for everyone who would live in relationship with God. The same was true with our Savior. In the Gospel according to Luke, he is particularly concerned with the prayer life of Jesus. Luke relates a couple of parables unique to his Gospel, not to be found in the other three gospels, and these relate to his emphasis upon prayer in Jesus' life.

The second of the secrets is also obvious. The early church was not only a praying church, it was a Pentecostal church. One has only to read the book of Acts to realize how significant a role the Holy Spirit played in the life of the early church.

Scholars have tried to analyze the book of Acts to structure and outline it in a number of different ways. One is to take the statement in the first chapter of Acts where Jesus says, "you will be my witnesses in Jerusalem, and in all Judea and Samaria, and to the ends of the earth" (v. 8). Luke carried as a motif in his writings the idea of movement. Luke's Gospel account is structured around the movement of Jesus toward Jerusalem. Beginning in chapter nine, Luke wrote, "Jesus resolutely set out for Jerusalem" (v. 51). Understand Luke is not speaking geographically at this point, for when you follow Jesus, He moved from Galilee down to Bethany back up into Galilee. Luke is making a spiritual statement.

Therefore, it would only be reasonable in the book of Acts, the second volume of Luke's writings, that movement would again be part of what he's trying to say. This time it is not movement toward Jerusalem, it is movement away from Jerusalem. The disciples moved from Jerusalem toward Judea, Samaria, and the remotest parts of the earth. The church is the greatest evangelical witness to Jesus Christ as Savior and Lord.

Main Character of Acts

We could also structure the book of Acts around the main characters. In chapters one through twelve we have St. Peter as the main character. Beginning in chapter thirteen the apostle Paul is the main character, and therefore the book is easily divided into those two segments. We have the apostle to the Jews, Peter, and the apostle to the Gentiles, Paul.

However, neither in Acts 1-12 nor in Acts 13-28 is the main character Peter or Paul. Throughout the book of Acts the main character is truly the Holy Spirit. A British New Testament scholar, Donald Guthrie, has suggested the book of Acts might well be renamed, not the Acts of the Holy Spirit, as some people call it, but rather the Gospel of the Spirit, because if Matthew, Mark, Luke, and John represent the gospel of our Lord, then the book of Acts represents the gospel of the Holy Spirit. One has only to enumerate the number of times the Holy Spirit is mentioned in separate incidents in the book of Acts (incidentally, it's forty-four different times) to know the Holy Spirit is the primary character in this book. Acts is the work of the Holy Spirit. It is not what men have accomplished, but what God, through the Holy Spirit, has accomplished through people. When I say the early church was a Pentecostal church, I'm suggesting that's not a big secret. All one has to do is read the book of Acts to discover the Holy Spirit is certainly the primary character in this record of the early church.

We've made a great mistake in dealing with the day of Pentecost, because we have dispensationalized it. When people approach the meaning behind the day of Pentecost, they refer to it as the birthday of the church. That's unfortunate for a couple of different reasons.

The People of God

First of all, people imagine the church never existed before the day of Pentecost. The people of God, or the *ecclesia*, are the "called-out ones." In the Hebrew Old Testament the reference is to the *kahaul*, "God's chosen." Again and again God worked in the lives of His people. He called them out. He chose them. He established them. It's not wrong to talk about the church in the Old Testament, because the Israelites are akin to the people of God in the New Testament. As Paul would say, one is a Jew who is not one outwardly, but a Jew who is one inwardly. Being a Jew is a spiritual reality—true in the Old Testament as well as in the New Testament—but not as easily recognized in the Old as in the New. God has established His church, not to be associated solely with the day of Pentecost.

When the disciples began walking with our Lord and they became involved with Him in ministry, we have a sense of the people of God. For years, theologians have referred to the day of Pentecost as the birthday of the church. They may be right and I may be wrong. We associate the church with Pentecost, but we don't often recognize its previous existence.

Secondly and more primarily, we have a tendency to take the entrance of the Holy Spirit inhabiting the people of God, and we place it at a time in the past as though it were a single event. We think it's only been accomplished in the past. That's unfortunate. We fail to realize God's gift of the Holy Spirit was not some dispensational act signifying the initiation of a new movement. Rather, it was part of the redemptive purpose of God. The gift of the Holy Spirit is not something done for the church at one time in history, but it is what God wants to do for the church in every period of history. You and I as individuals ought to expect to have the abiding presence of the Holy Spirit within our lives. We can expect the fullness of the Holy Spirit today as the early church experienced it. Unfortunately we lose the meaning when we make it an event that happened centuries ago.

Pentecost for Everyone

We in the twenty-first century have difficulty with the term Pentecostal church. It has come to be associated with a particular movement we refer to as Pentecostalism. That's also unfortunate, because Pentecost is not the sole possession of one denomination or a group of churches. Pentecost is God's purpose for all His people. If Baptists, Wesleyans, Episcopalians, and Roman Catholics are not Pentecostals, we have failed to realize a major and important part of God's redemptive purpose. When God gave the new covenant, it was not simply the promise of the Messiah, for that was only one aspect of the divine promise. We also have the promise of the gift of the Holy Spirit. Both of these gifts—the Incarnation and Pentecost—God included in the new covenant He wanted to establish with His people.

When people think of the fullness of the Holy Spirit, they associate it with a kind of emotionalism with which most of us don't like to identify. In the church we're too afraid of emotions and that's unfortunate. Some have said, "Brother, we're afraid of this wildfire." Most churches I've visited don't have to worry about wildfire. They should instead worry about freezing to death. We've become too sophisticated in our worship services; we view worship as stiff and formal.

When I spent a couple of summers in Jerusalem, I liked to attend the Scottish Presbyterian church near the Hinnom Valley. I enjoyed the preaching. Once I heard the pastor say, "The trouble with us

Presbyterians is we're starched and ironed without being washed." Without our being washed, God's great redemptive purpose is being frustrated in our lives. The Holy Spirit is not to be associated with an emotionalism that's uncontrollable and irrational. God doesn't work that way.

Pentecost and Other Tongues

Let's also dispel from our minds that Pentecostalism has to do with speaking in unknown languages. Let's speak the truth. As recorded in the book of Acts we read that on the day of Pentecost when the Holy Spirit came upon the church, they spoke with other languages. Those various people groups were amazed and basically said, "How can this be? We are Parthians, Medes and Elamites, dwellers of Mesopotamia, and we're visitors from Rome and other places, and yet we hear these people speaking to us in our own native languages. How can this be?" (See Acts 2:4–12.)

I believe God has a specific reason for interaction. Remember that in the book of Acts, speaking in other or unknown languages was not always the sign of receiving the Holy Spirit. In the eighth chapter of Acts when the Samaritans were filled with the Holy Spirit, there's no record about their speaking in any other language. When Ananias prayed for Paul to receive his sight and "be filled with the Holy Spirit" (9:17), there's no mention about Paul speaking in any other languages. He was indeed filled with the Holy Spirit. When you study the Bible, speaking in unknown tongues is not the necessary sign of being filled with the Holy Spirit.

If God wants us to speak in some other language, then by all means we accept His gift. As long as it is God who wants it and not people. If it is not manu-factured, then we don't have to be afraid of it. If God is the author, it will never be an embarrassment.

Pentecost and Miracles

A third misconception views the Holy Spirit in terms of miracles. In his book, *The Way to Power and Poise*, E. Stanley Jones[30] said the Holy Spirit is not a miracle monger, but a moral manager: "the manifestations of Thy Spirit are, not magical, but moral." Some people are mainly interested in the miracles and not too interested in the mor-als. Above and beyond all else the ministry of the Holy Spirit is an ethical ministry. One of the sure signs of the abiding presence of the Holy Spirit in any individual's life is that the Holy Spirit is sanc-tifier. His ministry is to make us a holy people. You and I are to be separated unto God and to be made like unto Him. There is no substitute, for the goal of every Christian is to have the mind of Christ. How can we then have the mind of Christ apart from the moral revolution the Holy Spirit can accomplish within our lives?

John Wesley said the most distinctive teaching of the Christian faith is the matter of original sin. At this point we stand in contradistinction to all other religions. Other religions see man as basically good. In Judeo-Christian faith the right assessment is that basically man is not good but fallen. Our native tendencies don't seek after God but tend toward selfishness. We know that left to ourselves we are a tremendously selfish lot. Apart from the ministry of the Holy Spirit, we could never be like Christ.

Notice this statement: "Now, Lord, consider their threats and enable your servants to speak your word with great boldness. Stretch out your hand to heal and perform signs and wonders through the name of your holy servant Jesus" (Acts 4:29-30). The footprints of God in the first century church witness to the reality of God. Those acts could not be attributed to human performance. God was at work, and we know it to be the touch of His hand.

Miracles are still possible today; God still performs miracles. At the same time, God is not going to entertain us with His performance of the miraculous. Nor is He going to do the miraculous so we can believe. If we cannot believe Him because of who He is, neither will we believe Him if we see a miracle.

Truth can be found in the story of Lazarus. In John's gospel, chapter 11, we read Jesus raised Lazarus from the dead. John recorded that *some* of them believed. When I was young and preaching revival services, I thought if some kind of miracle would happen, a great revival could break out. I don't believe that anymore. Even the miraculous will not convince most of us.

You see this in the fourth chapter of Acts. The Sadducees "seized Peter and John and, because it was evening, they put them in jail until the next day" (v.3). They confronted them about Jesus and the miracles He had done. They warned Peter and John never to preach in the name of Jesus. Notice how the members of the Sanhedrin conferred with one another: "'What are we going to do with these men?' they asked. 'Everyone living in Jerusalem knows they have performed a notable sign, and we cannot deny it'" (v. 16). Why would they want to deny it? Too often even the truth cannot be persuasive.

The Holy Spirit is a moral manager and not a miracle monger. Look at some of the positive aspects about the Holy Spirit.

The Promised Holy Spirit

First, the Holy Spirit is the promise of the Father to believers. Jesus said to the disciples, "'Do not leave Jerusalem, but wait for the gift my

Father promised, which you have heard me speak about. For . . . in a few days you will be baptized with the Holy Spirit'" (Acts 1:4–5).

In the Old Testament we identify several passages regarding God's promise of the infilling of the Holy Spirit. For example, on the day of Pentecost, Peter quoted from the prophet Joel: "'And afterward, I will pour out my Spirit on all people. Your sons and daughter will prophesy'" (Joel 2:28; Acts 2:17). We find the same promise in Isaiah: "'For I [Isaiah was speaking for God] will pour water on the thirsty land, and streams on the dry ground; I will pour out my Spirit on your offspring and my blessing on your descendants'" (Isaiah 44:3). Go also to Ezekiel, a favorite passage of John Wesley: "'I will give you a new heart and put a new spirit in you; I will remove from you your heart of stone and give you a heart of flesh. And I will put my Spirit in you and move you to follow my decrees and be careful to keep my laws'" (Ezekiel 36:26–27). We have here part of the new covenant God had promised. The gift of the Holy Spirit is for us all, the promise from the Father.

On the day of Pentecost the people cried out, "What shall we do?" Peter answered: "'Repent and be baptized, every one of you, in the name of Jesus Christ for the forgiveness of your sins. And you will receive the gift of the Holy Spirit. The promise is for you and your children and for all who are far off — for all whom the Lord our God will call'" (Acts 2:38–39). The promise was not only for them; it was for all believers in all times and in all places.

The promised Holy Spirit is for us now. God never intended for the church in the twenty-first century to win the world for Jesus Christ without the power necessary for the church in the first century. What He gave the first century church God gives to the twenty-first century church. What He did for an apostle Peter He wants to do for a John and Sam and Mary and Jane today. It's God's will for our lives.

A Personal Infilling

To be a Pentecostal church is to be a recipient of the promise of the Father, the gift of the Holy Spirit, and in terms of a personal infilling.

The secret of the early church was to be found in the fact they had personally experienced the Holy Spirit. In William Arthur's book, *The Tongue of Fire*,[31] he wrote about the problem he saw in the church, for many of the ministers of that day were preaching without the power of the Holy Spirit. Therefore, those ministers were frustrated and weak. Arthur pointed out that the problem we often have is a theology by inference rather than by consciousness. The world doesn't want to know what we infer about God; the world wants to know what we know about God.

J. Herbert Kane, former professor of missiology at Trinity Evangelical Divinity School, spoke in a chapel service at One Mission Society. He made a statement similar to this (as I remember it): "In America we're interested in whether something is true. But in most of the world they're not interested in whether it's true; they're interested in whether it works." I agree that many Americans aren't interested in knowing what our dogma is; they want to know whether it transforms lives. They want to know what can be experienced through Jesus Christ.

The disciples had a personal infilling of the Holy Spirit and that's what we need. Apart from the fullness of the Spirit, we cannot possibly be the church God has intended us to be. We need to be filled with the Holy Spirit.

Everett L. Cattell, Quaker missionary in India, became president of Malone College (1960–1972). In his book, *The Spirit of Holiness*,[32] he wrote that the Holy Spirit is like light. The quality of light is to fill the whole room, so when light comes into a room, shadows are created by those objects which block the flow of light.

We can't be filled with the Holy Spirit until we're willing to allow obstacles to be removed, for they cast shadows and keep light from filling every crack and corner of our lives. The only way we can be filled with God's Spirit is when we are willing to be emptied.

The poem, "Indwelling," by T. E. Brown,[33] speaks about being emptied. I quote:

> If thou couldst empty all thyself of self,
> Like to a shell dishabited,
> Then might He find thee on the ocean shelf,
> And say, "This is not dead,"
> And fill thee with Himself instead.
> But thou are all replete with very thou,
> And hast such shrewd activity,
> That when He comes, He says,
> "This is enow
> Unto itself – 'twere better let it be,
> It is so small and full, there is no room for Me."

With the indwelling of the Holy Spirit, we'll discover God is not only able, He is desirous of filling us like He filled the early church. It's a personal infilling, to be true within our lives. It's not a secret; it's clear in the pages of Scripture. Yet for us today, in many places and in many ways, this remains a secret from the church, a belief that used to be quite evident. It is God's will for the church to be filled with His Spirit.

The only way we can be filled is to be emptied of ourselves, for then we discover Pentecost is not simply the birthday of the church. It is a part of God's redemptive plan for every individual who would come to God through Christ.

I love the passage in Revelation about the great battle between the followers of God and the beast and his followers. I relish in all its symbolism. About the followers of God, the apostle John recorded, "They triumphed over him by the blood of the Lamb and by the word of their testimony; they did not love their lives so much as to shrink from death" (Revelation 12:11). When we are willing to be emptied of ourselves, we shall know the fullness of His Spirit. The church of today can still win the world for Jesus. A praying church. A Pentecostal church. That's what God has called each and every church to be today. God helps us to be all that He wants us to be.

Prayer: Our Father, thank You for the example of the early church. We know they were not perfect people and they did not do everything precisely right. We know they had faults and foibles the same as people of every generation. If we could go back, we could point out cracks in their vessels. At the same time, we realize the truth about the early church that made it the instrument of the Holy Spirit. By their example and pattern we find what You want us to be. Help us, our Father, to be a praying people. Help us to be a Spirit-filled people. For Jesus' sake, as well as for our own, we ask in His name. Amen.

They were a Pentecostal church. They were infilled by God's Spirit. It is then no great secret why that individual's life should be radically transformed and why that person should be useful in the work of God's kingdom.

Third, the early church was a proclaiming church, a vital part of being used of God in His kingdom. The church is God's witness to the world.

We've heard the anecdote about how someone talked to Jesus when he got to heaven and asked what His plan was for world evangelization. Jesus pointed to the disciples, and the person asked, "But what if they should fail?" Jesus responded, "I have no other plan." A nice story, but it's true. We, the church, are God's only plan for evangelizing the world.

God intended the Israelites to be a light to all the nations. From the beginning, God intended that His chosen people should be His witness to the world. It started back with Abraham. All the nations of the earth were to be blessed in Abraham.

Missions was God's purpose from the beginning. As Christians, if we don't understand about the vitality of missions for church life, then we've failed to understand the purpose of God. Our Lord chose those disciples. Under His tutelage, they received seminary training to be His witnesses. Jesus had no other plan.

Note how Luke begins the book of Acts: "In my former book, Theophilus, I wrote about all Jesus began to do and to teach" (1:1). Now here is volume two. The implication is all Jesus began to do and teach is now being completed. Being completed by whom? The disciples. They would literally carry through with the very ministry Jesus had begun. We see some tremendous implications. For example, in the whole idea of the atonement, it's implied in the concept of "participation in his sufferings" (Philippians 3:10). We are called not only to enjoy the benefits of Christ; we are called to participate in His sufferings. It's the challenge for those who are called to be His disciples today. Using Acts 4:29–34a, we focus on four ideas about being a proclaiming church, this business of being God's witness to the world.

"Now, Lord, consider their threats and enable your servants to speak your word with great boldness. Stretch out your hand to heal and perform signs and wonders through the name of your holy servant Jesus." After they prayed, the place where they were meeting was shaken. And they were all filled with the Holy Spirit and spoke the word of God boldly. All the believers were one in heart and mind. No one claimed that any of their possessions was their own, but they shared everything they had.

With great power the apostles continued to testify to the resurrection of the Lord Jesus. And God's grace was so powerfully at work in them all that there were no needy persons among them. —Acts 4:29–34a

Proclaim with Our Lips

First, the early church proclaimed with their lips the wonderful message of Jesus Christ. Of this we need to be reminded, for sometimes we fail to acknowledge that God wants us to bear witness to Him in different ways. One way is with our verbal testimonies. We are called to proclaim the Word of God with our mouths.

When those disciples came face to face with the threat against their lives, they did not get down and pray, "Oh Lord, you know these Sadducees, rulers of the Sanhedrin who threatened us. We pray you would send the Holy Spirit and wipe out this bunch of buzzards." I would have wanted to pray that way: "Lord, get rid of the opposition." What impressed me is they never said a word about the threat or those who were threatening them. Instead, their sense of responsibility was vital to the preaching of the Word of God.

There's a great lesson here. The greatest obstacles that exist in the proclamation of the Word are not those out there, but they are the obstacles within us. The greatest threat to the church today lies within the doors of the church itself. If we will be what we ought to be, then we can be light to our world. We can be a witness to those who sit in darkness, fulfilling the great task God has given us. "Faith comes from hearing the message, and the message is heard through the word about Christ. And how can they hear without someone preaching to them?" (Romans 10:17, 14). We proclaim the truth of God's Word.

Facing imminent danger, those disciples heard the threat against their lives, and they prayed, "Enable your servants to speak your word with great boldness" (Acts 4:29).They desired to be faithful in the proclamation of the Word of God. The church today has the same task. God has called us to bear witness to Jesus. Consider two facts evident in the lives of those disciples.

What Christ Has Done for Me

First of all, they bore witness to the resurrection of Jesus Christ, their primary significance. Their responsibility was to give witness to the fact that they beheld with their eyes the Christ who had been crucified and resurrected from the dead.

Second, the disciples gave their own personal testimonies. "With great power the apostles continued to testify to the resurrection of the Lord Jesus" (Acts 4:33). Notice two aspects: the objective truth that Jesus was raised from the dead and they were witnesses to what they had seen.

What is the job of a witness? It's not to give a projection as to what might have been; the job of a witness is to tell what he knows as fact. In the introduction to his first epistle, the apostle John wrote, "That which was from the beginning, which we have heard, which we have seen with our eyes, which we have looked at and our hands have touched—this we proclaim concerning the Word of life" (1 John 1:1).

In their case, it was the physical resurrection of Jesus, but it was also their own personal word of testimony. Remember: "They triumphed over him by the blood of the Lamb and by the word of their testimony; and they did not love their lives so much as to shrink from death" (Revelation 12:11). The word of testimony is a vital part of any Christian witness. Proclaiming the word of God is truly important for the church today. In measure at least, our testimony is the declaration of what God has done within our own hearts and lives.

The only testimony we can give to the world is what God has done within us. You might say, "I'm not a preacher. I've not gone to seminary. I don't have any great training. I'm not a good speaker." But the greatest witness we can bear is simply to tell what is true in our own lives. What has God done for you? What is God doing now within your life? The most important witness for you and me as Christians is to have a vital, contemporary, up-to-date relationship with Jesus Christ—in order to talk about what He is doing right now.

Being around testimony services, I've noticed people get up and say, "I thank God fifteen years ago Jesus Christ became my personal Savior." Wonderful, but what's happened in those fifteen years?

It's like marriage. I can tell you that in 1957 on August twenty-fourth, Ann and I repeated our wedding vows in Mobile, Alabama. But if that's the only declaration I can give of our marriage, you'd have to admit I don't have much to say. I make a distinction between a wedding and a marriage. A lot of people have weddings, but all do not have marriages. A wedding you can perform in a matter of minutes in the sanctuary of a church or in the office of a justice of the peace, but a marriage takes a lifetime. A marriage is what you build in day-by-day relationships. That's also true of our relationship with Jesus Christ.

I don't downplay our momentary experiences, because we need those. We need the point in time when we accept Jesus as Savior and Lord. We know when we've made that kind of commitment, that life-changing decision. We've established a covenant with Christ the same as we did in marriage. I stood at the altar of the chapel of Spring Hill Avenue Methodist Church in Mobile, Alabama, and at four o'clock in the afternoon of August the twenty-fourth, 1957, I entered into a covenant. It's real, and it means a great deal to me.

An awareness of my relationship with Jesus Christ happened the moment I established a covenant with my Savior. Yes, I have entered into covenant with Him. He is my Savior, because I've surrendered my life to Him. I know I have done that. And everyone reading this should know their own commitment. I don't, however, put much stock insisting you have to remember the precise time and place. It's like the husband who never can remember which day or year he got married. As long as he knows he's married and has a good marriage, it's not important he remember the date. What's important is having a living, vital relationship.

The same is true in our relationship with Christ. It isn't necessary to name the exact spot or time, but we must know today that we have entered into a covenantal relationship and we have surrendered our lives to Christ. The first-century church was a proclaiming church, and the first essential they had and you and I have is to proclaim Jesus Christ as *my* Savior. Secondly, He is *my* Lord. Those need to fit together.

Now how are we going to proclaim the truth of the Gospel? First of all, we do it with our lips. We've got to speak our witness of Christ to others. We need to tell everyone. People say that's not important. It's the expression, "What you do speaks so loudly I can't hear what you say." But we have no substitute for the spoken word.

I think back to those conversations when my parents were alive. I can still hear in my inner ear the way my dad answered the telephone. He's been dead since 1974, but I can still hear him. When my mother was living, we would generally call her on Saturday mornings. I can still hear her words. I cherish those precious moments. The same is true in our interpersonal relationships. We need to speak those words of truth and love. The disciples wanted to speak the Word of God, and we want that also. But it's not enough.

Proclaim with Our Lives

Secondly, the disciples proclaimed not only with their lips but with their lives. Whatever we say with our mouths is inconsequential unless it's corroborated with our lives. I've been told I have preached great sermons, but if when looking at my life you never saw any verification of what I said, it would not mean anything. Someone said preaching is not the making of a sermon and delivering it, but it's the making of a preacher and living it out. A preacher is no more than the life lived. When I stood in the pulpit, what difference did it make unless my life confirmed my message?

The same is true for every one of us. Unless we proclaim with our lives, our speech is lacking truth. Look at the early church for an example: "All the believers were one in heart and mind. No one claimed that any of their possessions was their own, but they shared everything they had" (Acts 4:32). How did they proclaim? They proclaimed with their lives in several different ways.

The early church had unity of purpose, one heart and soul. We misinterpret that if we assume it meant they agreed on everything. At one point Paul and Barnabas disagreed so strongly they went separate ways. Only insecure people need to have an environment where they always agree and say the same thing. The mark of genuine maturity is when we're able to live together by accepting our differences. Only an immature person wants to be a clone of someone else or for others to be a clone of him. Because God has made us differently, it ought to cause us to rejoice in this kind of fellowship. However, while we may not agree on everything, we need to have unity of purpose.

When I was academic dean at Asbury College, I read statements from educators that the time was rapidly coming when small Christian colleges or small independent colleges would be wiped out because of lack of students. Educators told us the survival of the small college in this day and time was not a good likelihood. If any institution was going to survive, then it had to remember its reason for existence. Otherwise, it would find itself a victim of the times.

The same prediction could be true of a church. What ought to be the absolute foundation of a church board's actions is to decide why the church exists. What is our purpose? Why are we a church? All we do should fit into the purpose of why we exist. It's true in a spiritual sense. What is our goal? Christians ought to be committed to the idea of being what God wants us to be. Unity of heart and soul is our witness to the world. We proclaim with our lips, and we proclaim with our lives also.

Love Relationship

In the first-century church they had a harmony of relationship, and it ought to be true of us today. Jesus said, "By this everyone will know that you are my disciples, if you love one another" (John 13:35). Is that true for us as a church, the body of Christ, today? Our lives demonstrate the love of Christ to a world in which love is lacking.

Wherever a church shows love for one another, people will pound on the doors to be part of that kind of community. When we are a loving community, we accept people in their brokenness, accept people with all their problems and difficulties, and make them understand they are loved because God loves them. It's important to show why God loves you and me. Not for what we can do, but for who we are—the way we love each other is not with ulterior motives.

I read again W. E. Sangster's great book, *The Pure in Heart*.[35] Sangster cited one of the problems in missions is our failure to understand we are to love people simply because they are people made in the image of God. We're not to love them in order to convert them. The minute we do that, we have made love impure, tainted. If we love others only because of what we can do for each other, then that's imperfect love. Where we reach out and show true love "without condition, without bargaining," that is the greatest proclamation of what we ought to be.

The early church proclaimed with their lips, their lives, and their love. Notice: there was not a needy person among them. Such as any had needs, the church ministered to them (Acts 4:32–36). Isn't it tragic now we want the government to do what the church used to do? The church once accepted upon itself the responsibility of caring for those who were needy. Instead, now we stop and analyze the needy. We say they ought to do this and that, and all may be true. If God had stood back and looked at my life and said, "Bill Coker ought to do this and he ought to be a better person before I will love him," then I would have been lost. But God loved me.

Paul wrote, "God demonstrates his own love for us in this: While we were still sinners, Christ died for us" (Romans 5:8). We proclaim with our lips; we proclaim with our lives; and we proclaim with our love.

Free To Be

Lastly, the early church proclaimed by their liberty. They were free—free to be what God had intended them to be. One of the greatest witnesses we could give the world today is the fact we are free in Christ. We are not bound by people and traditions. We're not bound by people's expectations. We're free to be what Christ intended us to be. Make no mistake about it, we are not to be insensitive to people. What it does mean is we are free because Christ has set us free.

You say, "Where do you see that in the passage?" I see it beautifully when Peter and John stood before the Sanhedrin and they looked back at them and said (in my words), "Friends, do with us whatever you feel you have to do, whatever you need to do. But we can't be bound by what you think. We can do nothing else but speak in the name of Jesus." In their proclamation even death had lost its terror. They were free in Christ, free even to die without being afraid of dying. When that's true, friends, we have proclaimed to the world the message of what Jesus taught us about eternal life. They were a proclaiming church with their liberty. They proclaimed Jesus as Lord. We are His people. And we are the recipients of His benefits.

I don't know about you, but I long to see the church as a proclaiming church—preaching God's Word, not ours. Jesus is the only Savior of the world. I'm more interested in what Jesus has to say than what any theologian spouts. Jesus has the words of eternal life. Men don't have that word.

Therefore, I want to proclaim God's Word, not mine, not yours, not some theologian's. Jesus died for the sins of the world. It's His word, and I want to speak His word. I want to do more than talk about it; I want it to radiate out of my life. I want it to be reflected in the love He gives me; I want to be free to be His person, controlled only by Him. Somehow I believe if we in the church could reflect God's love, then the church would be the church for today's world.

If you have a tendency to criticize the church sometimes, remember one simple statement. The church is never any more than, or any less than, the people who make it up. The church is not a building. It could burn down tomorrow, and you haven't lost anything eternally. Because the church is you; the church is me. You learned it in math class: the whole is the sum of the parts. A church is the sum of the people who form the body of Christ. If we're a praying people, if we're a Spirit-filled people, if we're a proclaiming people, the world is waiting for us because the world is waiting for Jesus. You and I are the ones to present Christ to them.

Prayer: Father, thank You for time in Your Word. How we wish out of these pregnant ideas all the implications would flow. Our only prayer is for all of us to go out as proclaimers of Jesus Christ with our mouths, with our lives, by our love, and by the fact that Jesus Christ has made us free to be His people and to live for Him in the midst of a needy world. If we can do that, Father, then we believe we can be the church of Jesus Christ, in whose name we pray. Amen.

CHAPTER NINE

To Be His Holy Bride

Ephesians 5:25–27

"To seek to be different from other churches is to become competitive and humanly creative. To seek to be a holy people is to fix our sights on God and to be open to His purposes" (W.B.C.).

Many people today don't take the church seriously, but I know Jesus took the church seriously. Read what Paul said to the church (or to churches) in the book of Ephesians, the fifth chapter:

Christ loved the church and gave himself up for her to make her holy, cleansing her by the washing with water through the word, and to present her to himself as a radiant church, without stain or wrinkle or any other blemish, but holy and blameless.
—Ephesians 5:25b–27

In that same chapter Paul wrote about a profound truth: "For this reason a man will leave his father and mother and be united to his wife, and the two will become one flesh. This is a profound mystery" (Ephesians 5:31, 32). This refers to Christ and the church.

In the hymn, *The Church's One Foundation*, Samuel Stone[36] echoed Paul's thought in the first stanza: "From heav'n He came and sought her To be His holy bride." Suggested here are two considerations about Christ and the church, and I trust they will speak as forcefully to you as they have to me.

Faith's Object Is Christ

The first consideration is the personal nature of our faith: to be His holy bride. It's personal because the object of faith is a person. When we talk about Christian faith, we mean something more than an intellectual or religious conviction. Yes, we often categorize Christian faith as a religion, but it's more. Ever since the incarnation of Jesus Christ—the Word becoming flesh and living among people, being seen, heard, and touched, and with whom His disciples shared precious moments and years—Christianity has never been identified as a religion or an intellectual conviction. The incarnation is central to our faith because it focuses our attention upon a person. The person of Jesus Christ, God manifested in the flesh, came and sought for Himself a bride. If we were to press through and discuss the various aspects of Christian theology, we would ultimately have to come back to the fact that the object of the Christian faith is a person.

These days people are talking about the ministry of the Holy Spirit and well they should, because Jesus had promised the disciples that His leaving would be to their advantage so the Holy Spirit could come. People often refer to the Holy Spirit as an *it* or a power or a force, but the Holy Spirit is a person. We bow here before the absolute mystery of the character of God, three persons in one. The Spirit is among us, more than the influence of God in the midst of His creation, more than the power of God as He flexes His sovereign muscles to say He is God. Beside him there is no other. The Holy Spirit is the person of God, not simply present in the world but present in the lives of people.

What's beautiful about Pentecost is not how God gave us some kind of great power to surge through our spiritual lives, but God gave Himself to take up residence within our lives, to be real inside of us. This is a mystery we cannot begin to explain, for the reality of the one who abides within us personally is God Himself. The temple of God is no longer a beautiful place in Jerusalem; it's no longer a majestic tent built to symbolize the presence of God in the midst of the Israelites; but it is God resident in the human heart. The person of the Holy Spirit dwells in us as persons.

Christ came to seek us to be His holy bride, wrote Samuel Stone in his hymn, but I want you to see in those words the personal relationship: the object of the bride's affection is the person of God Himself. Not a conviction, not believing in supernatural power or religion, but a person. It's personal not only because the object of our faith is a person, but because we who are involved in faith are persons. How could it be impersonal if you and I as persons are involved in exercising faith?

Elevation of Individualism

Another matter of faith surfaces. Today we've elevated the idea of individualism. It's the idea that we can have and maintain faith apart from the body of Christ, the church, apart from fellowship with others. These ideas depart from Old and New Testament faith. Yet in too many instances, church leaders have overemphasized the idea of our relationship with God as an individual one. It's a personal relationship, but in the New and Old Testaments it's not an individual one.

Because we have elevated individualism we've seen some disastrous results within the kingdom of God on earth. For example, it's led to the devaluation of the church. What I've heard from pastors is that the church is not significantly valued in the minds of their congregation, those who call themselves followers of Christ. We have lost the value of the church and our emphasis has been placed upon the individual. In people's minds the church is thought as an option. "Well, you know, I'll catch it if I can, but if I can't, it's no real problem." Oh, but there is a real problem!

Think about the Olympic Games. I've always appreciated and followed athletics. I've not only been involved in sports, but our three sons and our daughter actively participated in team and individual sports. Some performances are for individuals when a person literally stands on his or her own, getting onto the bar or beam or mat. Our sons were wrestlers. What a serious moment it is when a young man prepares to go out on the mat and he's the only one with his competitor. His teammates are on the sidelines. Whether he wins or loses depends on what he alone does. Some sports emphasize the individual.

However, many athletic games are built on the spirit of the team. When you have too many prima donnas, you don't end up with a team; you end up with great individuals. There's a great danger with the dream team. The church is like an athletic team. Whenever we devalue the idea of the body of Christ, whenever we lose sight of the possibility that our togetherness might be swallowed up by individualism, then we have forgotten something the Old and New Testaments strongly emphasize.

The Israelites had no individual relationship with God apart from the nation of Israel and yet theirs was a personal relationship. In the New Testament those who followed Jesus understood that while they came to a personal God and exercised personal faith, their relationship was never an individual matter. They were part of His body and He was the head and they were the body together, the bride for whom He had come and given His life. In the church today the emphasis of individualism exists at the expense of the body of Christ, and it has led to the devaluation of the church, locally and universally.

Power and Relevance

Individualism has also moved the church to be powerless and irrelevant. The church is no longer considered a powerful force with which people must reckon, and that ought to disturb everyone. There was a day when politicians, keenly aware of a dynamic in the church, could afford to dismiss it only at their peril. Today few politicians con-sider the church to be of any great power in the United States, let alone in the world. And, what of the church's relevance? Do we have a signifi-cant role in our local communities, cities, and country? Do people realize if the church ceases to be, we will lose from our society and from our civilization one of the most dynamic influences for good the world has ever known, and our lives substantially will be lessened because of the fail-ure of the church?

If we went out into our individual communi-ties today, we would find people who don't see the church as relevant. As I've listened to my wife talk about her volunteer work at a crisis pregnancy center, I've picked up that among those young peo-ple who come in, they don't see much significance to the church. Some may admit belief in God, but it's rather abstract. Now the burden is upon us, because as followers of Christ we should not accept the fact the world has written us off.

We ought to seek for that kind of relationship with Christ, not only on a personal basis, but as the body of Christ, for then we could once again have a dynamic voice in our world and certainly in our communities. The church needs to speak about the evils of the day, because if we do not, our country will hear only silence. Unless the church is offended by the wrongs done to people, unless we are incensed by what's contrary to our righteous and holy God, who then is going to be actively involved in healing and help? Do we expect the conventions of political parties to wax eloquent about righteousness and holiness? No, we're not that foolish.

I'm realistic about what has happened, but I'm optimistic in believing the power of the living God is still available if the church will be the church. If we understand Christ has claimed us as His holy bride, then together the body of the Christ can make a difference. Until the church begins to be valued seriously, then it's going to continue to be viewed as powerless.

Dog and Pony Shows

I'm concerned about the ministry today. I attended seminary between 1960 and 1965 and we were concerned about what was happening in the ministry then. In my own denomination I pastored for three years before going to seminary and I watched as pastors vied for the better appointments in the conference. It all boiled down to how popular you were and how well you could be received. That became the litmus test, not genuine spirituality relayed by the power of the Holy Spirit operative in a pastor's life. It came down to dog and pony shows then, and I fear it's still true of the ministry in the church today.

The pastor who puts on the best show, the pastor who produces the best entertainment, can expect to draw the biggest crowds. If you think I'm spouting untruth, then you're ignorant of the church today. Whence come many of these megachurches? Do they come out of great revivals or do they come out of what more they can offer? Why does a pastor go to Las Vegas to study from nightclub entertainers, to discover how best he can put on a show? This was reported in the *Wall Street Journal* a number of years ago. Why has the church been sold as another style of entertainment? Isn't it because we have not taken the church seriously?

Our focus upon individualism has been an over emphasis. Nowhere in Scripture do we find any suggestion that you and I can make it into heaven all by ourselves. We need the body of Christ. While our faith is personal and it cannot be anything other, we also recognize our church, the body of believers, belongs to Christ.

Personal Relationship

What does it mean when we say our religion is both personal and communal? Are we talking in contradicting terms? Are personal and church mutually exclusive? I don't think so. Our faith is personal in the sense it is internal and subjective, as a bride feels intensely that personal moment when she walks down the aisle of the church to be greeted by her intended and to exchange their vows. In the same way, we have a personal relationship with God. Paul strikes at the heart of this in his letter to the Romans: "A person is not a Jew who is one only outwardly, not is circumcision merely outward and physical. No, a person is a Jew who is one inwardly; and circumcision is circumcision of the heart, by the Spirit, not by the written code" (2:28–29a). That's a personal relationship. The personal relationship a bride has with her groom is akin to the personal relationship a believer has with the Lord.

I grew up in the Methodist Church. Our particular species of that denomination was liberal. We failed to focus upon a personal relationship with Christ. In all my early years attending church, no one ever challenged me to accept Christ as my personal Savior. I never attended a revival service where an evangelist challenged people to commit themselves to Christ. Our church had an impersonal quality. As children we went through a membership class and joined the church. As I reflect back on those days, the church was deficient in some serious ways, but it was the mother of my spiritual life. It was in that church I heard

God call me into ministry. It's not my intention to write off my church, but rather to emphasize how easy it is for any church to become impersonal.

The last church I pastored focused its attention on a great missionary program. How different that was from the church of my youth where mission giving was only an item in the general budget, a slice of the pie. In all my growing up days, I never saw a missionary. They were sort of out there in the middle of somewhere.

In my last church we rejoiced over our mission program being personal. We invited missionaries to come; we gave to specific missionaries, and we posted their pictures on the board with a map to show where they served. But such a program can still be impersonal. How easy it is to write a check and on the memo line put "mission budget." I played my pledge; I've done my share. Yet we may not have entered into any kind of intercessory prayer for the people to whom we are giving support. How heavily do we carry them on our hearts? How personal is our relationship with our missionaries?

Missions can be impersonal. Giving to missions might reveal one gaping exception. We've given our money, but have we offered up our sons and our daughters to Christ? In our homes do we encourage our children to know what could be the greatest fulfillment in their life—not to have a great job and make a lot of money—but, if God should call them, to offer their lives in service to His kingdom? If you and I don't offer them opportunity to serve, then we are impersonal in this business of missions.

Do you see what I'm driving at? We are not to wrap ourselves up in our own sense of Christ's righteousness so that we never see the need of being together the body of Christ. Never should we come to the place where our giving to the kingdom of God is something we routinely do with a check in the plate and never with flesh and blood and never with genuine concern. It should be personal; personal because each gift says commitment. I must make it my involvement with the kingdom of God. No one else can do it, whether helping in Vacation Bible School or as a Sunday school teacher or singing in the choir. "It is my church and I belong. I am involved." That's personal.

There are no cheap seats in the grandstands for the kingdom of God. We can't sit back and trust others will do the work. The church will make a difference in our day only because people care enough and are committed enough and are willing to participate enough to make the church what it ought to be by the power of the living Christ.

I have no great wisdom as a human being. If the Holy Spirit is not present in the words of a sermon, all efforts are in vain. But if the words of Scripture can come alive through the presence of the Holy Spirit, then He can make a living contribution in someone's life. I am also aware it doesn't happen unless I am willing to be involved, willing to be committed and help it happen. It's true of pastors; it's true of every last one of us.

One year at our last church we had about one hundred sixty-five children attend Vacation Bible School, but it wouldn't have happened if those fifty adults had not participated. Some of them had menial jobs. They poured the punch or cleaned up behind the crafts. Maybe they didn't do anything of great significant, but because they were there, Vacation Bible School took place. That's true of the church at large in every aspect of its outreach. We don't reach out and make a difference in the community unless there is personal contribution.

Christ's Holy Bride

"From heav'n He came and sought her to be His holy bride" (Samuel Stone). As personal a moment as it is for a bride to stand at the altar of the church and say, "I do," it's as personal when you and I come and look into the face of our Savior and say, "I do."

The second major consideration about Christ and the church is the matter of holiness. We seek to be Christ's *holy* bride. The centrality of holiness is evident in all of Scripture. You cannot talk about a relationship with God apart from holiness. Holiness is there on every page, in every book, and in every letter. To the extent that the church fails to be holy, it fails to be the bride for whom Christ gave Himself. It's important for us to understand that.

We've been given a simple truth: holiness is not a theological doctrine. It's a way of life. I gave many years of my life to being a professor. I don't for a minute regret I had those classes with my students, explaining theology, what we believe. I find no room in the church for a nebulous fuzzy-headed type of thinking about what we believe. But more and more we say to people in the church that it isn't theology, it's the life. You and I can believe all of the right doctrines, but unless our lives practice what we believe, nothing else matters. It's both: believing the right precepts and living the right way. I am convinced all the more that unless in our way of living we incorporate the great power of God through the indwelling presence of the Holy Spirit, you and I are only spinning our wheels.

Often I've said the best seat in the church at a wedding is not the ones reserved for the bride's mother or the groom's mother. As the officiating pastor I've had the best place, for I stand and look into the faces of those two people exchanging their vows. It is such a precious moment; nothing interferes. Sometimes I've had to hold back my own emotions even for people I don't know well. Their mutual love is significant when they look into each other's faces and say their vows. It is indescribable.

At its heart, holiness means belonging. Belonging to Christ, being His and saying "I do." Christ gave Himself for the church that He might sanctify and cleanse her. We are the church; we are His holy bride. We are the ones for whom Christ offered Himself. If I am part of the church, and if Christ with His own blood has bought me and for my life He died, then my prayer is for God to help me be part of the church without spot or wrinkle or any such thing. In the apostle Paul's second letter to the church in Corinth, he wrote about the bride of Christ: "I promised you to one husband, to Christ, so that I might present you as a pure virgin to him" (2 Corinthians 11:2).

We are to be the kind of church that belongs to Christ, one that makes a difference in the world. Friends, you and I are not going to make it by ourselves. God never intended us to be loners. He always intended we should be part of the church. Whenever you and I allow the church to be devalued in any way, either by our lack of participation or concern, we strike at the heart of the message of redemption in the New Testament.

Holy Communion

I don't know of anything in the history of the church more important than the celebration of Communion. It is the focal point of togetherness. It is who we are as the body of Christ. That's why ritual grew up around the Lord's Supper. It was more than church leaders wanting to formalize it. They wanted to come to the place where the church together might celebrate its relationship to the living Christ.

I'm aware our differences do mark us, for some of us come out of various backgrounds, but my prayer as we take Communion is to realize that when we affirm our faith we do it as the body of Christ. This is what we believe, and when we pray together and consecrate the elements, we do it as the body of Christ.

We come to the Lord's Table, and He invites all who repent of their sins and are at peace with their neighbors, who intend to lead a new life by following the commandments of God and walking in His holy ways, to be a part of this celebration.[37]

In the early church this celebration took place with joy, yet with great seriousness. In Paul's first letter to the Corinthians, you find these words in the eleventh chapter:

The Lord Jesus, on the night he was betrayed, took bread, and when he had given thanks, he broke it and said, "This is my body, which is for you; do this in remembrance of me." In the same way, after supper he took the cup, saying, "This cup is the new covenant in my blood; do this, whenever you drink it, in remembrance of me." For whenever you eat this bread and drink this cup, you proclaim the Lord's death until he comes (1 Corinthians 11:23b–26).

Prayer: "Father, hallowed be your name, your kingdom come. Give us each day our daily bread. Forgive us our sins, for we also forgive everyone who sins against us. And lead us not into temptation" (Luke 11:2–4). Amen.

CHAPTER TEN

Unity: the Church's Priority

John 17

"What good is all our busy religion if God isn't in it? What good is it if we've lost majesty, reverence, worship—an awareness of the divine? What good is it if we've lost a sense of the Presence and the ability to retreat within our own hearts and meet God in the garden? If we've lost that, why build another church?" (A.W. Tozer, *The Attributes of God I*).[38]

I invite your attention to the seventeenth chapter of John's Gospel, at the conclusion of the upper room discourse, a passage we all know well. We call it the high priestly prayer of Jesus. Read through the whole chapter, for it is beautiful, and not that long.

After Jesus said this, he looked toward heaven and prayed:

"Father, the hour has come. Glorify your Son, that your Son may glorify you. For you granted him authority over all people that he might give eternal life to all those you have given him. Now this is eternal life: that they know you, the only true God, and Jesus Christ, whom you have sent. I have brought you glory on earth by finishing the work you gave me to do. And now, Father, glorify me in your presence with the glory I had with you before the world began.

"I have revealed you to those whom you gave me out of the world. They were yours; you gave them to me and they have obeyed your word. Now they know that everything you have given me comes from you. For I gave them the words you gave me and they accepted them. They knew with certainty that I came from you, and they believed that you sent me. I pray for them. I am not praying for the world, but for those you have given me, for they are yours. All I have is yours, and all you have is mine. And glory has come to me through them. I will remain in the world no longer, but they are still in the world, and I am coming to you. Holy Father, protect them by the power of your name, the name you gave me, so that they may be one as we are one. While I was with them, I protected them and kept them safe by that name you

gave me. None has been lost except the one doomed to destruction so that Scripture would be fulfilled.

"I am coming to you now, but I say these things while I am still in the world, so that they may have the full measure of my joy within them. I have given them your word and the world has hated them, for they are not of the world any more than I am of the world. My prayer is not that you take them out of the world but that you protect them from the evil one. They are not of the world, even as I am not of it. Sanctify them by the truth: your word is truth. As you sent me into the world, I have sent them into the world. For them I sanctify myself, that they too may be truly sanctified.

"My prayer is not for them alone. I pray also for those who will believe in me through their message, that all of them may be one, Father, just as you are in me and I am in you. May they also be in us so that the world may believe that you have sent me. I have given them the glory that you gave me, that they may be one as we are one — I in them and you in me — so that they may be brought to complete unity. Then the world will know that you sent me and have loved them even as you have loved me.

"Father, I want those you have given me to be with me where I am, and to see my glory, the glory you have given me because you loved me before the creation of the world.

"Righteous Father, though the world does not know you, I know you, and they know that you have sent me. I have made you known to them, and will continue to make you known in order that the love you have for me may be in them and that I myself may be in them."—John 17

When we read this prayer, it's rather obvious, isn't it, that Jesus had several concerns on His heart as He faced Calvary? He had those last moments with His disciples while He prepared Himself to be an offering, a sacrifice for the sins of the world. Jesus first dealt in terms of His own relationship with the Father. He had completed the work God had given Him, ready to go back to the presence of the Father: to assume again the glory He had before the foundation of the world, the glory He shared equally with God.

Second, we are aware that Jesus bore a burden for those who had been with Him through the past three years. He had given them the Word of God. They had responded in faith to that Word and had come out of the world to follow Jesus. Now Jesus had a great burden on His heart for those people. So He prayed for the disciples, preparing them to carry the gospel to every creature.

Third, He prayed not only for those who had gathered there with Him in the upper room, but

He knew others would believe in Him. So He prayed for the extended church—not only the ones immediately present with Him but included those who would come to be His followers through the word the disciples would share. He prayed for the church at large.

Jesus had a burden for the church. It was a fledgling church, only getting started and about to be confronted with the most difficult task ever to be given human beings. Jesus was going back to the Father, and they would take up the responsibility of preaching the gospel to all people everywhere in the world. Sharing the good news of the kingdom of God and bringing people to faith in God would not be easy, and Jesus knew that. So he carried a great burden as He prayed for them and for the extended church.

I'm writing now about the church's priority, and it's unity. I have reasons for suggesting this is a priority, because in Jesus' last prayer for His disciples, four different times He specifically addressed the question of their unity. He was concerned that they should be one.

Pattern for Unity

I lift up several related causes on the matter of unity as we discover it here in this beautiful prayer. First, I suggest the pattern for unity you find in Jesus' words. It's simply put. He prayed "that all of them may be one, Father, just as you are in me and I am in you" (v.21). That's the pattern. As the Father and the Son are one, then all who name the name of Jesus Christ are to be one. But what does that supposed to mean? God the Father and God the Son are one in a specific sense. What we understand about the doctrine of the Trinity is that the Father, the Son, and the Holy Spirit are three persons in the unity of one substance. Obviously, Jesus wasn't talking about the disciples and us being such a unity. He did not say they should be in any sense some kind of a single substance with a trinity of personality. We need to understand what Jesus meant when He said, "that they may be one as we are one" (John 17:11).

What occurs to me (and I don't make any contention for it being the last word) is we can suggest some verifiable truths. For example, we could observe several facets about the Father and the Son regarding their unity into which we *can* enter and participate. For example, we look at the Father and the Son and we know by way of Scripture that they are one in the light. They are one in truth. In First John, chapter one, John wrote about our walking in the light as God is in the light (v. 7). In that sense our unity is in the light as they are in the light. So we are to be unified in the light that God gives: the light of the knowledge of the truth of God.

Jesus gave to the disciples the word of truth. He shared the Word of God with them; He broke the truth to them. He had let the light of God shine upon their lives and, in essence, said, "Father, as you and I are unified in the light of the truth, I pray for these people, that they shall be unified in the truth."

This doesn't have to stretch our imaginations, because as we read through this prayer, we note the many times Jesus talked about the truth and its significance. We pay particular attention to God the Father and God the Son as light. Thus we are to be unified in that light.

For a second aspect we go again to the writings of John. He wrote that God is love. In his first epistle, John got rather exercised about this business of love. John wrote that God is love and the one who abides in love abides in God, and God abides in that person. (4:16). That's exactly what Jesus meant in His prayer.

They were to have a oneness brought on because they were walking in the light as God is light, and as the Father and the Son have a relationship of love, we also are to enter into that same kind of relationship. We are to have a oneness born out of love. What a tremendous word for us: we are to walk in the love of God, for walking in that love we find unity.

A unity of purpose also exists between the Father and the Son. Jesus prayed about God having sent Him into the world for a specific purpose. His mission was to bear witness to the truth that all men might come to the knowledge of the truth. There is a redemptive purpose in Christ. When we observe in the Bible about the Father, Son, and Holy Spirit, we see again and again a unity of purpose. There's a unity of labor, if you please.

Jesus said that His meat was to do the will of God. Thus He prayed that His people would be one as He and the Father are one in purpose. It's not only a oneness of light and a oneness of love, but a oneness of purpose. The Father and the Son are bound together for the redemption of the world, so Jesus prayed that His disciples should be one in that same pattern of oneness. We hear Jesus saying we should be one like that.

Extent of Unity

Now, let's take a second step. We've seen the pattern for our unity. The second aspect we notice is about the extent of the unity between the Father and the Son and the church. What do we mean by the extent of unity? Let's go back to the prayer and listen to what Jesus said. First, that they may *all* be one. That's the extent of the unity. Here are the disciples—eleven of them who have remained true to Jesus Christ—and Jesus said in His prayer to the Father that the extension of unity may be such as to incorporate *all* people into a oneness. Not one is to be left out, not one is pushed aside. Jesus was talking more than about the eleven. Others had followed Him, and we can say this prayer included all of those people as one.

Now the extension of unity is unto all people. Stop and think about that. We make a lot of distinctions in the church, don't we? We make distinctions between clergy and laity. But when you go back to the Gospels, we don't read about any such distinction being established by Jesus. And when we go to the book of Acts and the Epistles, we discover that while people may have different functions and while God may use them, if you please, in different offices, there never was a suggestion of difference between one and the other. All people are bound together in unity, and God does not make any particular distinctions.

We make a habit of thinking that religious leaders are a certain category of people who fill offices. But who are the unreligious then? Here is where some false distinctions are made. Oneness does not create a barrier between clergy and laity, yet it's too easy for us to do that within the church today.

We create other kinds of barriers in the church. We create barriers between males and females. We say there's a distinction at this point, but Paul said no. He said that in Christ, all are the same; all are one. We make distinctions between various kinds of social strata, but God doesn't recognize those. The bond and the free are altogether one in Christ. (See Galatians 3:28.) Regrettably, we too often build on these various distinctions.

I have a set of slides on Jerusalem prepared by an English medical doctor who became a professional photographer. In one scene, he made a statement that suits our study. He talked about how Jerusalem, the old city, is surrounded by the wall, but he adds that even within the city there are a number of other walls.

When I spend a summer in Jerusalem, every day I got away from the institute and I walked through the old city, absorbing the atmosphere and the culture. I allowed my mind to go back though the history of Jerusalem. Walls within walls. It's not only a wall separating Jews from Muslims or Christians, but you go into the Christian section and there are more walls within walls that separate Armenians and Anglicans. Walls are built everywhere.

We do that today. Throughout the history of the church we find walls built between Catholics and Protestants. Go back before that. We find walls between Eastern Orthodox and Western Orthodox. Now we find walls between Presbyterians, Baptists, Methodists, Episcopalians, Christian Reformed, and Pentecostals. We set up walls, and we have to wonder: where is the unity that is ours in Christ? Differences of understanding and biblical interpretation create some of the distinctions of our groups, and not all of these reasons can be blinked away.

Christ prayed that unity within the disciples should extend to all people, and not one of them is left out. He wanted all of them and us to be one, not only His disciples. Christ prayed for the church—those who did believe as well as those who would later believe—and so the extension of unity comes right down to our own day. Christ looked out upon the church and prayed, "Father, that they may be one." I emphasize that when Christ prayed for the church, unity was a priority. And unity today has to transcend all of the distinctions we make among those who believe in Christ.

What then is the extent of the unity? If the pattern of our unity is oneness, as the Father and the Son are one, and if the extent of our unity is for all of us to be one, let's ask one other question. What are the means of our unity? Jesus prayed, "I have given them the glory that you gave me, that they may be one as we are one—I in them and you in me—so that they may be brought to complete unity. Then the world will know that you sent me and have loved them even as you have loved me" (John 17:22–23).

Complete Unity

So, what's the means of unity? To blow your mind, I suggest what Jesus meant in His prayer is that the means of unity within the church is *perfection*. I didn't make that word up: "that they may become perfectly one" (v. 23, KJV). The verb states they may become perfected as one. The idea behind this word primarily has to do with the sense of wholeness and completeness, as the NIV states: "brought to complete unity." How can there be unity in the church? Jesus said the only way of producing unity in the church is through the accomplishment of a wholeness, a completeness, or to use that word "perfectness" within the church.

What does that mean? First, perfection has to do with the reuniting of a divided heart. Our hearts are divided when we fail to walk as God wants us to walk. But when we come into the light of His truth and seek to walk according to the will of God, He takes the broken pieces and brings them together into oneness.

How can we ever be one with one another unless we are one within ourselves? If I am divided within myself, there's little hope of my being one with you. And if there are divisions within ourselves, we can't expect there to be a unity within the church. So what do we need? We need unity to take place, and that can only happen, first of all, by the uniting of my divided heart and your divided heart.

The psalmist wrote about this in Psalm 86. Listen to his words. "Teach me your way, Lord, that I may rely on your faithfulness; give me an undivided heart, that I may fear your name" (v. 11). Evidentially the psalmist thought there was a division within himself; for he couldn't come to the place where he would reverence the name of God, to respect and stand in awe of God's name, until his own heart was unified. I suggest, first of all, that the perfectness of which Jesus prayed comes out of the reunification of our hearts.

A second point is a restoration of the *integrity* of the heart. The heart is not only divided, the heart is also fallen. Sin has made its inroads; destructive forces are evident. If there's to be a oneness, I need not only for my own heart to be reunified in God, but also restored. What's needed is integrity, an essential completeness and wholeness before the presence of God. Go to Psalm 101, where David wrote so beautifully: "I will sing of your love and of justice; to you, Lord, I will sing praise. I will be careful to lead a blameless life—when will you come to me? I will conduct the affairs of my house with a blameless heart. I will not look with approval on anything that is vile" (vv. 1–3).

"Blameless" means integrity of heart. That word *tāmam* in Hebrew is our word for perfectness. It's the same word we find translated in Greek as perfection, completed, or blameless in John 17:23. David said in Psalm 101 that until he walks before God in the blamelessness of his conduct—integrity of heart—he cannot be perfect before God.

The means of accomplishing unity within the church is this matter of perfecting the heart. First of all, reuniting the heart, second, restoring the integrity of the heart, and third, it means *reestablishing love* in the heart.

What's the one thing we know about sin in the heart of humanity? We can easily respond. Sin, in its essence, is selfishness. Doesn't it reflect that we have lost love? Rather than my concern about others, I have placed myself—to use Bill Bright's figure in his little book on being filled with the Holy Spirit—I have placed ego/self upon the throne. If I'm bowing before my ego, if I'm exalting myself, then I cannot choose others, because to choose someone else means I have to repudiate self. That's the conflict, isn't it? Until my/your heart is reestablished in love I/you cannot possibly expect to be unified with our brothers and sisters in Christ.

We read this in Jesus' Sermon on the Mount. Listen to Him in chapter five of Matthew. "But I tell you, love your enemies and pray for those who persecute you, that you may be children of your Father in heaven. . . . If you love those who love you, what reward will you get? . . . And if you greet only your own people, what are you doing more than others? Do not even pagans do that? Be perfect, therefore, as your heavenly Father is perfect" (vv. 44–48).

It's interesting to me how people go through different kinds of gymnastics to get away from that word "perfect." But we can't change the text, can we? It's still there. Jesus said we are to be perfect as our Father in heaven is perfect. And when you put it in context, He was not suggesting for a moment that you and I could live flawless lives. The whole point of this passage is that love should prevail, and it is a love that does not draw lines between friends and enemies. It is a love that reaches out to the just and to the unjust, to the good and to the evil; it is a love that reaches out to all people.

We see a demonstration of that love in the Good Samaritan who had every reason in the world to be hostile to that Jew lying there in the dirt. After all, the Samaritans were often mistreated by the Jews, and the Samaritans also mistreated the Jews. It was not a one-way street, yet this man came along the road and spotted a man who was not one of his own. Traditionally they were enemies, yet he reached out in love. (See Luke 10:25–37.)

Summary

We cannot be an exception to the Lord's injunction to reestablish our hearts in love. In summary, what is it we need if we are to be a unified people? First, we need to be reunited in our divided hearts. Second, we need to be restored in the integrity of our hearts, for our fallen hearts need to be restored. Third, we need to be reestablished in love, because our hearts are sinful. Jesus said in His prayer: Father, I pray that these My disciples might be one even as We are one.

Two more principles are necessary if those disciples were ever going to be one. Number one: Jesus prayed that the Father would protect them and keep them from the world that hated them and from the evil one. If they were to maintain that unity, they needed to be protected. Number two, Jesus prayed that they should be sanctified through the truth, for only as they were made holy through the truth could they be made one.

That's the thrust, the focus, of Christ's prayer for His disciples then and now.

Prayer Target

Plan in your devotions to read again this prayer from John's Gospel and reflect on Jesus praying for you. Ask yourself: What is Jesus seeking? As you take this prayer to heart and think about it, ask: If Jesus were praying for the church today, what would He say to us? Also, What is Jesus saying to me personally? I think you'll agree with conviction that whatever else Jesus said, at the top of the list, He prayed for His people to be unified in the Father as He and the Father are one.

CHAPTER ELEVEN

Let the Church Be the Church

Preparing the Church for Today
1 Peter 1:22—2:10

"The unique thing about the early Christians was their radiant relation to a Person. . . . It was this engrossment with a victorious Person that gave verve and vibrancy to their lives and conviction to their testimony" (A.W. Tozer, *The Root of the Righteous*).[39]

Sometimes the difficulty in reading Scripture is due to breaking into what an author intended as a continuous account or letter, and when we pull out a passage we lose its context. I begin with the first chapter of First Peter, verse twenty-two, and conclude with chapter two, verse ten.

Now that you have purified yourselves by obeying the truth so that you have sincere love for each other, love one another deeply, from the heart. For you have been born again, not of perishable seed, but of imperishable, through the living and enduring word of God. For, 'All people are like grass, and all their glory is like the flowers of the field; the grass withers and the flowers fall, but the word of the Lord endures forever.' And this is the word that was preached to you. Therefore, rid yourselves of all malice and all deceit, hypocrisy, envy, and slander of every kind. Like newborn babies, crave pure spiritual milk, so that by it you may grow up in your salvation, now that you have tasted that the Lord is good. As you come to him, the living Stone—rejected by humans but chosen by God and precious to him— you also, like living stones, are being built into a spiritual house to be a holy priesthood, offering spiritual sacrifices acceptable to God through Jesus Christ. For in Scripture it says: 'See, I lay a stone in Zion, a chosen and precious cornerstone, and the one who trusts in him will never be put to shame.' Now to you who believe, this stone is precious. But to those who do not believe, 'The stone the builders rejected has become the cornerstone,' and, 'A stone that causes people to stumble and a rock that makes them fall.' They stumble because they disobey the message – which is also what they were destined for.

But you are a chosen people, a royal priesthood, a holy nation, God's special possession, that you may declare the praises of him who called you out of darkness into his wonderful light. Once you were not a people, but now you are the people of God; once you had not received mercy, but now you have received mercy. —1 Peter 1:22—2:10

When I was a sophomore in college, a district superintendent from the denomination in which I grew up approached and asked if I would be willing to pastor a small church in LaPlace, Louisiana. A heady assignment for a nineteen-year-old boy, but in my naïveté and self-assurance, the challenge did not overwhelm me at all. I'm no longer a naïve college boy, and I'm not so self-assured anymore. In all honesty, pastoring a church is an overwhelming assignment.

Changes, Opinions, Differences

We need to prepare the church for the future, but many changes have occurred in the church over the past 2000 years. Some changes have been good and become part of a normal development of the church. We can't anymore go back to the first century church than we can go back and re-create the nineteenth century in America. We live in a world of change, so changes are needed if the church is going to be the church and minister to people today.

Not all changes, though, have been good. The church has suffered from wrong choices. Think particularly of the medieval era when the church was placed in the hands of the clerics, the professionally religious, and laypeople basically became spectators. We don't want to go back to that period of time when laymen were uninvolved. Laypeople would find themselves missing out on the blessings of God and the church failing to be the church.

Many opinions surface about what we ought to be and what we ought not to be and how we ought to conduct ourselves and how we ought not to do it. Many opinions represent the personal preferences we have or the traditions from which we have come. These differences make the church in the twenty-first century struggle a great deal more in the effort to be the church and minister to people. Our preferences vary one from the other, and our traditions are so different we have to grapple with the problems they generate.

Gordon MacDonald wrote a book entitled *Forging a Real World Faith*,[40] and he examined six instincts in people. They can be referred to as styles of worship that represent our opinions. First of all, there are people who follow the *aesthetic* instinct.

The keyword for them is majesty. These people prefer beauty, order, and tradition.

Second, MacDonald suggested some people have the *experiential* instinct, and their keyword is joy. They want to feel the presence of God, to be free and sense the excitement of worshiping God.

A third group are those in whom the instinct is one of *activism*. The keyword for these people is achievement. They aren't excited about sitting around doing nothing—as we mostly do at church. After all, we live in a world with such desperate need, so we ought to be up and doing. Let's get busy.

Then there's a fourth group. MacDonald referred to this as the *contemplative* instinct. These people are different than the activists; their keyword is listening. They want to sense God's presence, to discover the inner light of communion with God.

As a seminary student, I went to a Trappist monastery in Kentucky. None of the monks spoke. Silence was the vow. They went to bed every night at seven o'clock and got up every morning at two o'clock to begin the day's worship. As a seminary student who felt like he understood most of what God was all about, I thought: What a waste of time. Why do they even want to do it? My friends, the church would be much the poorer if we lost the contributions of those mystics and all they came to know about God in their contemplations.

Fifth is the *student* instinct group. For these people the keyword is truth. For them worship ought to be time to study the Word of God. It's all about coming to sense God's will. They want a pastor who's going to declare the unsearchable riches of God. How tragic if in the church we lost the quest for truth.

The sixth and last group Gordon MacDonald mentioned is those for whom their *relational* instinct is most important. Their keyword is love. They want the worship service to be one of bonding the community in the fellowship of love, a sense of mutual support. They like to hold hands and hug each other.

Now I don't know if Gordon McDonald has exhausted all of the various categories, but you and I can identify with several of these groups, and we have preferences. Some of us would rather die than stand around holding hands, and others love to sing the *Doxology*: "Praise God from whom all blessings flow,"[41] while still others ask why we sing this every Sunday. We are different people and we worship differently.

In the midst of all these difficulties and differences, we deal with theories about how we need to prepare the church for today. With all of the new marketing techniques and exhortations to "get with it" or "be relevant," I sometimes feel uncertain, inadequate, and unconvinced. On more than one occasion, I've felt like saying, "Let's go do something else." But if Christ loved the Church and gave Himself for it, there is no way I nor you can love Him without loving the Church for which He died.

Personal and Corporate Factors

So how are we going to make these forces work in spite of our differences and in the face of a rapidly changing world? How is the church going to be the church? In this first epistle of Peter he said what is as appropriate today as when he wrote it. His teaching could be as helpful for us in being the church today as it was helpful for the early church when they sought to be what God had raised them up to become. Peter gave basic truths, bottom-line principles, if the church is going to be the church.

As I've reflected on this passage, I noticed what I never saw at other times, even though I have read it often and again. It's as if I saw this truth for the first time; it's simply the personal factor. The apostle wrote, "come to him, the living Stone—rejected by humans but chosen by God and precious to him" (1 Peter 2:4).

What I hadn't noticed before is the next verse: "you also, like living stones, are being built into a spiritual house" (2:5). Jesus Christ is *the* living

Stone. But you and I, as members of the church, are to be like Him; we are ourselves to be living stones, and we are to be built into a church. What a strong emphasis upon the personal element of the church!

I believe firmly the church does not belong to any denomination. It does not belong to any group of elders and deacons. It does not belong to any one human being. It belongs to God. It is His Church. But at the same time, the Church of God is composed of persons who have come into a personal relationship with Christ.

I am reminded of what Paul said in his letter to the Ephesians. He wrote, "You are no longer foreigners and strangers, but fellow citizens with God's people and also members of his household, built on the foundation of the apostles and prophets, with Christ Jesus himself as the chief cornerstone. In him the whole building is joined together and rises to become a holy temple in the Lord. And in him you too are being built together to become a dwelling in which God lives by his Spirit" (Ephesians 2:19-22). We are to be living stones, built together, formed and fashioned into a holy temple indwelt by the Spirit of God.

The personal factor is that we have been chosen, and as living stones, we are meant to be a holy priesthood, offering spiritual sacrifices acceptable to God through Jesus Christ. Paul wrote about that in the fourth chapter of Ephesians. God has gifted people differently, for He calls apostles, prophets, pastors, and teachers. Those gifts and functions exist, but the church does not belong to the clergy.

Every believer has the right of access into the presence of God. In the Protestant Reformation, emphasis on the priesthood of all believers became the chief cornerstone of the revolutionary doctrine of the Reformers. Along with the right of access into the presence of God comes the responsibility of offering the sacrifice of worship. In order to be like living stones ourselves, pay attention to the personal injunctions. These injunctions are necessary in our personal lives if the church is going to be the church and if we are going to belong to God.

Injunctions for the Church

I give you an outline on this passage and you can develop your own thoughts. At the beginning of chapter two in First Peter, the apostle said, "rid yourselves of all malice and all deceit, hypocrisy, envy, and slander of every kind" (2:1). In other words, Peter is saying to those people and to us: personal relationships have to be cleaned up. The church can never be the church if we allow personal relationships to become bankrupt, and if we let differences separate us from one another, keeping us from being living stones, formed and fashioned into a spiritual temple. So how do we deal with that?

First of all, Peter is saying, if the church is going to be the church, it has to make sure the personal relationships established across differences never permit malice and deceit, insincerity, envy, and slander to break down the mortar binding us together in Christ.

Second, Peter wrote that we should "crave pure spiritual milk, so by it you may grow up in your salvation" (2:2). Note what he said. Personal ambitions need to be spiritually oriented. People all over the world have goals and purposes which do not reflect the presence of the living God. They may be secular; they may be materialistic; they may be self-indulgent. But if the church is going to be the church, our personal ambitions must be cast aside, those which splinter the church and keep it from being all it ought to be.

Third, Peter exhorted, "abstain from sinful desires, which wage war against your soul" (2:11). One great mark about being the church is that our personal discipline needs to control our fallen tendencies. Certain people might think themselves better than others, but those of us who by the Spirit of God have been given a degree of honesty know we're not different from one another. It's not as though only *some* of us have ungodly tendencies not pleasing to God, for we *all* know we need to confront our faults and shortcomings. Personal discipline is something we have to engage in or else our fallen tendencies triumph over our best intentions.

Fourth, maintain good conduct among unbelievers. Peter said it this way, "Live such good lives among the pagans that, though they accuse you of doing wrong, they may see your good deeds and glorify God" (2:12). Personal practices have to be above reproach. If the church is going to be the church, then its representatives cannot be a reproach to the world. We are reliving Christ if we are living stones ourselves, cast in the image of the living Stone, the Son of God Himself. We don't let the world determine what is right or wrong, but our lives need to be consistent or else the church cannot be the church.

Fifth, for the Lord's sake we are subject to human institutions. "Submit yourselves for the Lord's sake to every human authority" (2:13). Personal politics must be governed both by what's right and the overarching truth that, after all, there is only one sovereign and He is God. We are placed in a world where personal relationships are not simply necessary, they are absolutely vital. So how do we deal with politics? Peter said we need to be governed by what is right and all our politics are under God's sovereignty.

Sixth, "Live as free people, but do not use your freedom as a cover-up for evil" (2:16). Personal integrity has to reflect personal redemption. We don't live as though we are bound by issues like those who don't know Christ, as though we are victims instead of conquerors through Christ. We need to live as free, but never allow freedom to compromise our personal integrity. Never is freedom an excuse, a license or special privilege for evil.

Finally, Peter said: "Show proper respect to everyone, love the family of believers" (2:17). Personal social graces should give evidences of God's grace. We are not a political party. We are not a social movement. We are the church of the living God, a people purchased by Christ on Calvary. We will never be the church unless these personal factors become real and manifest in our lives. Both the personal factor and collective factor abide in the worshiping community.

Principles for a Spiritual House

Peter mandated four principles in this passage if the church is going to be the church. First, as the body of Christ we must have centrality of worship. Notice what Peter said: "you also, like living stones, are being built into a spiritual house to be a holy priesthood, offering spiritual sacrifices acceptable to God through Jesus Christ" (1 Peter 2:5). The central function of the church is to worship God, to be captivated by His presence, to bow before His sovereignty, to love Him for who He is, and to rejoice in His work among us and within us.

To repeat, we are all different—coming out of distinct traditions, having varied backgrounds and diverse personalities. If each one of us could have the worship service exactly as we want, think what a mess it would be. We cannot expect complete agreement about how people should worship. But I'm convinced no worship will take place in any congregation unless we focus upon the centrality of Christ, unless we are caught up into the majesty of His presence, unless we sense Someone greater than the pastor stands before us and moves among us.

In the Protestant tradition we placed the pulpit in the center of the church. Its placement is a strong theological statement, for we believe the Word of God is central to the worship of God's people. The proclamation of His Word is a major component of all true worship.

On the other side of the coin, we are not a people who worship a book. We are a people who worship a Person. We worship God. Far more central than the written Word is the incarnate Word, and far more important than what a pastor says about the Word is the presence of Christ Himself. We cannot experience real worship unless we are brought into His presence.

In his book, *Evangelism Through the Local Church*, Michael Green[42] wrote: "Formal religion is as dull as dishwater." That may be true, for we're supposed to be alive, but it's more than noise and activity. However we worship, we must come with a sense of expectation and the stirring of the deepest emotions of our hearts because we are in God's presence.

Second, along with the centrality of worship must be a focus on mission. Peter wrote: "you are a chosen people, a royal priesthood, a holy nation, God's special possession, that you may declare the praises of him who called you out of darkness into his wonderful light" (1 Peter 2:9). Declare His wonderful deeds. Declare His praises. Declare His miracles. However the Greek word is rendered here, it's the mission of the church to declare, to pronounce, to publish, to proclaim what God has done in and for us.

We must not allow *mission* to be limited to evangelism or overseas missions. In most churches whenever we talk about missions we always think of overseas missionaries, but the mission of the church is bigger, broader, and deeper than that. I quote Michael Green at a place where I find myself compatible with him: "(Mission) embodies the total impact of the church on the world: its influence; its involvement with the social, political, and moral life of the community and nation where it is placed; its succor of bleeding humanity in every way possible" (*Evangelism Through the Local Church*).[43]

The mission of the church is as much of the concern and feeding of the starving masses of Somalia as it is sending a missionary to preach the gospel. It is as much a concern for the social and political structures of our nation as it is the maintenance of a worship service and the preaching of the gospel. We cannot separate the two— worship and mission—they go together.

Third, there must be an atmosphere of love and acceptance. Quoting the prophet Hosea in the Old Testament, Peter wrote: "Once you were not a people, but now you are the people of God" (1 Peter 2:10a). As the redeemed of every age have been God's people, so we recognize the gospel reaches out into our own age with the good news for those whom God loves and calls to Himself. In the church, there must be a sense of love and acceptance. We all come to God on the same level ground.

The fourth is that we must exhibit an attitude of concern. "Once you had not received mercy, but now you have received mercy" (v. 10b). We are a people who care for one another. We have received mercy and recognize others are also recipients of God's mercy. It may have been Charles Haddon Spurgeon who defined evangelism as "one beggar telling another beggar where to find bread." In the same way, concern is one person who has discovered the mercy of God telling another person where mercy can be found.

My friends, that's not the pastor's job. You did not hire your pastor to be concerned for all the people in the community. How can one person be concerned about all members of the church? The pastor loves you but can't carry everyone's concerns. So how are we going to do it? There's only one way it'll ever be done. It's when we all become agents of God's great compassion. No church will possibly serve as it ought unless we form within the church small groups who sense love and concern through close-knit fellowship. The challenge is upon us.

The pressure is on the church today to reach out into a world that's increasingly secular, into the midst of such deep, dark, and desperate needs in people. Can the church be the church? Every day we discover whether or not we can deliver the goods depends on whether or not the church is truly the church in our community.

Let's Build a Church

I'm thoroughly turned off by how we're led to believe a new marketing technique is going to save the church. I've asked myself how we can build the church, and I came up with a set of unique building plans.

We first of all lay a foundation strong enough in its theology and deep enough in its faith, so the burdens and weight of the real world can be borne. Second, we need to build a sanctuary large enough where all the different people and the multitude of differences among us can all meet together. Third, we need to build an altar that's central and beautiful, so every time we come to worship, our focus and our thoughts are not on a man but on God himself and on all of His grace and all of His love and all of His majesty.

In my floor plan for a church there are no walls. We need a church where anybody and everybody can feel welcome to come in. Walls would also prevent us from seeing everything around us.

Next the church has a magnificent electrical system, because it's to be lit by the glory of the presence of God. As in the book of Revelation, there will be neither sun nor moon in the holy city, because God and the Lamb are the light thereof. Could it be we don't need any human lighting in the church, for the glory of the presence of God lights up the place for us?

We don't need a heating unit, because we are to be warmed by the fervor of our love for one another. In the midst of a cold, dark world, we love one another fervently and in the warmth of love we find comfort. We also don't need an air conditioning unit, because a continual breeze blows through this sanctuary, and the wind of the Holy Spirit of God moves with Pentecostal gale winds, keeping us cool.

Lastly, this magnificent architectural plan is expandable in every direction. If ever such a church existed, people would desperately want to come within, because their needs are met there. Hidden behind much of what's being said today, the desire to come together is truly present. As Augustine[44] said long ago, "Thou hast formed us for Thyself, and our hearts are restless till they find rest in Thee." There's only One who can fill the emptiness, and He's God Himself.

We have this weighty challenge, and I want to tell you, it scares the life out of me. How do we build a church for the twenty-first-century? Above and beyond all desires, I suggest we build by keeping before us this one simple truth: the church must be the church and it can't be anything else.

Prayer: Our Father, we pray that You would stir our hearts to want to build Your kind of a church—the kind in which people can come with all our differences, with all our similarities, with all our likes and dislikes, and with all our preferences and ambitions. For we find at the foot of the cross of Christ only one cause transcending all else—the great love of God shed abroad in our hearts through the Holy Spirit. Thanks be to Jesus Christ who gave Himself for the Church. Guide us, we pray, and stir our hearts. Through Christ our Lord we ask. Amen.

Endnotes

I. Chapter One: *The Central Focus of the Church*

1. A. W. Tozer, *The Set of the Sail* in *The Pursuit of God Bible,* (Hendrickson Marketing, LLC, NIV, 2011, © Biblica, Inc.), 1326.

2. Charles Taylor, *Sources of the Self,* (Cambridge: Harvard University Press, 1989).

3. A. B. Simpson, Presbyterian pastor and founder of the Christian and Missionary Alliance.

4. Evelyn Underhill, *Worship,* (Third Edition, London: Nisbet & Co, 1951), 74–75.

5. Henry Blackaby, "We Need Revival," Interview with Nancy Leigh DeMoss Wolgemuth, Revive Our Hearts radio program. www.reviveourhearts.com

6. Power Evangelism, reported in a book by the same name, author John Wimber. For more information see: https://en.wikipedia.org/wiki/Power Evangelism

7. Diogenes Allen, *Christian Belief in a Postmodern World,* (Louisville: Westminster John Knox Press, 1989).

8. "When I Survey the Wondrous Cross," lyrics by Isaac Watts (1707).

II. Chapter Two: *Preparing a Church*

9. A. W. Tozer, *The Pursuit of God* in *The Pursuit of God Bible,* (Hendrickson Marketing, LLC, NIV, 2011, © Biblica, Inc.), 1125.

10. Council of Nicaea, AD 325. https://en.wikipedia.org/wiki/First_Council_of_Nicaea

11. The Council of Chalcedon in AD 451, https://en.wikipedia.org/wiki/Chalcedon

III. A. Chapter Three: *The Body Taking Shape*

III. B. Chapter Four: *The Body of Christ*

12. Pelagian. Pelagianism is defined as holding that persons are "born essentially good and capable of doing what is necessary for salvation." For a good explanation from a Wesleyan perspective: https://www.seedbed.com/consider-john-wesley-neither-pelagian-nor-augustinian/

13. George F. Will, "Forget Values, Let's Talk Virtues," (May 25, 2000, *The Washington Post*), https://www.washingtonpost.com/archive/opinions/2000/05/25/forget-values-lets-talk-virtues/0749a88f-e999-4830-8c58-c4b8394d524b/?noredirect=on

14. Tony Snow (1955-2008), White House Press Secretary, https://en.wikipedia.org/wiki/Tony_Snow – and Jesse Helms (1921-2008), United

States Senator; https://en.wikipedia.org/wiki/
Jesse_Helms

15. Philip Yancey, *Where Is God When It Hurts?*
(Grand Rapids: Zondervan, 1990).

III. C. Chapter Five: *One Body in Christ*

16. Patch Adams, MD, founder of Gesundheit!
Institute, Hillsboro, WV. *House Calls*, (San
Francisco: Robert D. Reed Publishers, 1998).

17. Bishop Lesslie Newbigin, *The Finality of
Christ*, (Richmond: John Knox Press, 1969), 92-98.
This is a paraphrase summation in which Newbigin
emphasizes the essentialness of the finality of
Christ and the need for conversion.

18. John R. W. Stott, *Between Two Worlds*, (Grand
Rapids: Wm B. Eerdmans Publishing Co., 1982),
51–58.

19. "Bind Us Together," lyrics by Bob Gillman
(1977).

20. "God of Grace and God of Glory," lyrics by
Harry Emerson Fosdick (1930).

21. Underhill, *Worship*, 226–227

22. "He Is Lord," lyrics based on Philippians
2:10–11.

IV. Secrets of a Dynamic Church

IV. A. Chapter Six: *A Praying Church*

23. William Arthur, *The Tongue of Fire* or *The True Power of Christianity*, lectures delivered to preachers, (Nashville: E. Stevenson & F.A. Owen, Agents for the Methodist Episcopal Church, South), 109. (Published also by Seedbed, 2014.) gospeltruth.net/tongue_fire.htm

24. Paul E. Little, *Know Why You Believe*, (Downers Grove, IL, InterVarsity Press, 1988), 152.

25. Oswald Chambers, *My Utmost for His Highest*, (New York: Dodd, Mean & Company, 1935), 173, 241, 291.

26. The Apostles' Creed, *The Methodist Hymnal*, 1939, (Nashville: The Methodist Publishing House), 512.

27. W. E. Sangster, "Covet Earnestly the Best Gifts," recorded sermon at Asbury Theological Seminary, (Wilmore, KY: Asbury University Duplicating Service, #77–116).

28. "'Tis So Sweet to Trust in Jesus," lyrics by Louisa M.R. Snead (1882).

IV. B. Chapter Seven: *A Pentecostal Church*

29. A. W. Tozer, *The Price of Neglect* in *The Pursuit of God Bible,* (Hendrickson Marketing, LLC, NIV, 2011 © Biblica, Inc.), 1312.

30. E. Stanley Jones, *The Way to Power and Poise,* (Nashville: Abingdon Press, 1949), 83.

31. Arthur, *The Tongue of Fire*, 69, 151, 215, 265–266, 285.

32. Everett L. Cattell, *The Spirit of Holiness*, (Kansas City, Beacon Hill Press, 1963).

33. Thomas Edward Brown, "Indwelling," poem first published in 1875 in *Plain Talk* under title "No Room." https://allpoetry.com/Indwelling

IV. C. Chapter Eight: *A Proclaiming Church*

34. A. W. Tozer, *The Set of the Sail,* in *The Pursuit of God Bible,* (Hendrickson Marketing, LLC, NIV, 2011 © Biblica, Inc.), 1326.

35. W. E. Sangster, *The Pure in Heart*: *A Study in Christian Sanctity*, (London: The Epworth Press, 1954), 245.

V. Chapter Nine: *To Be His Holy Bride*

36. "The Church's One Foundation," lyrics by Samuel J. Stone (1868).

37. Ritual for the Lord's Supper, *The Methodist Hymnal*, (Nashville: The Methodist Publishing House, 1939). Invitation: "Ye that do truly and earnestly repent of your sins, and are in love and charity with your neighbors, and intend to lead a new life, following the commandments of God, and walking from henceforth in His holy ways, draw

near with faith, and take this holy Sacrament to your comfort; and devoutly kneeling make your humble confession to Almighty God," 528–529.

VI. Chapter Ten: *Unity: the Church's Priority*

38. A. W. Tozer, *The Attributes of God I* in *The Pursuit of God Bible,* (Hendrickson Marketing, LLC, NIV, 2011 © Biblica, Inc.), 769.

VII. Chapter Eleven: *Let the Church Be the Church*

39. A. W. Tozer, *The Root of the Righteous* in *The Pursuit of God Bible,* (Hendrickson Marketing, LLC, NIV, 2011 © Biblica, Inc.), 1290.

40. Gordon MacDonald, *Forging a Real World Faith,* (Glasgow: HarperCollins, 1993; first printed in Nashville: Thomas Nelson, Inc., 1989), 87–113.

41. *Doxology*, lyrics by Thomas Ken (1674).

42. Michael Green, *Evangelism through the Local Church,* (Vancouver, BC: Regent College Publishing, 2012), 25.

43. Michael Green, *Evangelism through the Local Church,* 9.

44. Augustine, quoted by A. W. Tozer in *The Pursuit of God,* (Camp Hill, Pa., Christian Publications, Inc., 1993), 31.

Cf. Blaise Pascal, *Pensées* VII, 425, "What else does this craving, and this helplessness, proclaim but that there was once in man a true happiness, of which all that now remains is the empty print and trace? This he tries in vain to fill with everything around him, seeking in things that are not there the help he cannot find in those that are, though none can help, since this infinite abyss can be filled only with an infinite and immutable object; in other words by God himself."

Acknowledgements

When we start and end with thanksgiving, we have to give praise to our Lord Jesus Christ. He is the reason we pursue this publishing venture. We want to honor Him with our work and words. We work to please Jesus with our words, spoken and in print. These messages preached at World Gospel Church in Terre Haute, Indiana, covered several years. We believe deeply in the ministry of the church and have been blessed by members in many churches over our years of service.

When we found EABooks Publishing for Bill's second book, *Prayers for the People,* we did not hesitate to connect with them for the Advent book, *Scandal of Christmas.* Now with a third book, *Let the Church Be the Church,* we are grateful again for their expertise, faithful contacts, and patience with us. Thanks go to Robin Black, Cheri Cowell, Rebecca Ford, Jeanette Littleton, and Tanya Shanley (in alpha order). Others on staff who work behind the scenes.

We again used photos by Scott Kokoska taken at our 50th wedding anniversary. Thanks to Scott and his wife Carrie. In addition, I'm grateful for Donna Dene English who used her skills to convert a color photo into black and white.

We are especially grateful for Callie Daruk who transcribed the sermon tapes. Without her initial work, the book could not be published. We also appreciate those who read the manuscript and wrote the foreword and endorsements. Agreeing to that request took time from their busy schedules in ministries.

There are those whom we've never met—the authors of numerous books and references Bill used in preparing these messages. Check the endnotes to add to your learning experience.

Thank You, Jesus, for the opportunity and privilege to get Your written Word out into the world. We are grateful for our readers who digest the Word and live by it. God bless you all.

Pastor Bill and Ann Coker

About the Author

A native of New Orleans, Dr. William B. Coker, Sr., graduated from Tulane University in 1957. Answering God's call to preach, Bill pastored churches in Louisiana, Mississippi, Kentucky, and Indiana. Bill finished graduate programs at Asbury Theological Seminary (B.D. and Th.M.) and Hebrew Union College (Ph.D.). He served as assistant professor at ATS, professor of Bible and Greek at Asbury College (University) with two terms as Vice President of Academic Affairs. He also had two years as Vice President for Mission Advancement at One Mission Society.

Bill's last pastorate was World Gospel Church, Terre Haute, Indiana (1989-2008), and he worked on teams with the Emmaus El Shaddai community. After retirement, he assisted the senior pastor of Free Life Community Church (Wesleyan) in Terre Haute. Bill has three published books: *Words of Endearment: The Ten Commandments as a Revelation of God's Love*; *Prayers for the People: from the Heart of a Pastor*; and *The Scandal of Christmas: Advent Reflections on Four Unlikely Figures.*

Bill's wife, Ann L. Coker, serves as his editor and collaborator. They now live in Indianapolis, Indiana, and attend Southport Presbyterian Church. They have four grown children, ten grandchildren, and thirteen great-grandchildren. Ann graduated from Asbury College (University) twenty years after completing high school. Her editorial training came from working as managing editor of *Good News* magazine. She also contributed to *The Woman's Study Bible, NKJV,* Thomas Nelson Publishers. She writes for devotional publications, periodicals, and her blog (www.abcoker.blog). Currently Ann edits and compiles her husband's messages for publication and oversees his podcast: Words of Endearment with Bill Coker. Ann is a member of Heartland Christian Writers in Indianapolis.

Made in the USA
Middletown, DE
15 October 2022

12829708R00139